335.40924   A646   115897

Appelbaum, Richard P.

Karl Marx

SEP 1 8 '90

12-7-93

DEC 07 1994

DEC 0 8 1998

APR 2 0 1999

FEB 1 6 2000

Harrisburg Area Community College
McCormick Library
3300 Cameron Street Road
Harrisburg, PA 17110

D1293177

KARL MARX

MASTERS OF SOCIAL THEORY

Series Editor:

Jonathan H. Turner, *University of California, Riverside*

This new series of short volumes presents prominent social theorists of the nineteenth and twentieth centuries. Current theory in sociology involves analysis of these early thinkers' work, which attests to their enduring significance. However, secondary analysis of their work is often hurried in larger undergraduate texts or presented in long scholarly portraits.

Our attempt is to provide scholarly analysis and also to summarize the basic, core idea of the individual master. Our goal is to offer both a short scholarly reference work and individual texts for undergraduate and graduate students.

In this series:

KARL MARX

Richard P. Appelbaum

Masters of Social Theory
Volume 7

Cover Photo: Historical Picture Service

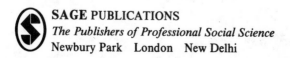

SAGE PUBLICATIONS
The Publishers of Professional Social Science
Newbury Park   London   New Delhi

Quotations from *Communist Manifesto, German Ideology, 18th Brumaire, Preface to Critique of Political Economy, Capital, volume I,* and *Class Struggles in France* are reprinted by permission of Lawrence and Wishart Ltd., London, England, and Oxford University Press.

Quotations from *Marx's Grundrisse* are reprinted by permission of A. D. Peters & Co Ltd.

Copyright © 1988 by Sage Publications, Inc.

All rights reserved. No part of this book may be reproduced or utilized in any form or by any means, electronic or mechanical, including photocopying, recording, or by any information storage and retrieval system, without permission in writing from the publisher.

For information address:

SAGE Publications, Inc.
2111 West Hillcrest Drive
Newbury Park, California 91320

SAGE Publications Ltd.
28 Banner Street
London EC1Y 8QE
England

SAGE Publications India Pvt. Ltd.
M-32 Market
Greater Kailash I
New Delhi 110 048 India

Printed in the United States of America

Library of Congress Cataloging-in-Publication Data

Appelbaum, Richard P.
    Karl Marx.

    (Masters of social theory ; v. 7)
    Bibliography: p.
    Includes index.
    1. Marx, Karl, 1818-1883. 2. Communism.
I. title. II. Series.
HX39.5.A5595   1988   335.4′092′4   88-4619
ISBN 0-8039-2579-4
ISBN 0-8039-2580-8 (pbk.)

SECOND PRINTING, 1989

Contents

115897

This book is dedicated to my parents, Theodore and Sylvia, who taught me to seek out the rational kernel; and to my children, Sara and Jason, who, I hope, have benefited as a result.

Series Editor's Introduction

As an anxious series editor, I have waited and waited for this book. And I am certainly glad that I did, for Richard Appelbaum has produced a beautifully written and well-argued analysis of Karl Marx's thought. Aside from presenting Marx's basic ideas, which is the prime goal of the series, the author has set Marx's thinking within a much broader intellectual, biographical, and social context. The end result is, I feel, a masterpiece of summary, interpretation, and contextual analysis.

Probably the most persistent theme throughout the book is the debate over the prospects for scientific sociology and the uses of scientific knowledge. On the surface, Marx appears to have been somewhat ambiguous on the status of scientific laws and the implications of lawlike tendencies for human agency, but Appelbaum clarifies Marx's position in simple terms: The structural tendencies—of a particular economic epoch, such as capitalism—constitute obvious constraints on human options and actions, but the crisis-producing contradictions in such structural arrangements create opportunities for human agency. In Appelbaum's words, "Marx did not treat human beings as blindly following universal laws. . . ."

Cutting across this debate on the nature of science and its uses is a detailed analysis of the context in which Marx's ideas first emerged and then matured.

For a rather short book, then, there is much packed into these pages. Yet, unlike so many books that seek to do much in little space, the reading is not dense. Indeed, it is remarkably smooth and flowing, even with the thorough analysis that it contains. For these reasons, I am delighted to add this stimulating volume to the Sage series on Masters of Social Theory. It represents not just an important addition to the series, but also marks a significant contribution to the large literature on Karl Marx's thought.

—*Jonathan H. Turner*

Preface

Marxism in the United States: A Rediscovery

Marxism, arguably the twentieth century's most influential social theory, remains largely unknown in the United States.

One-quarter of the world's population currently lives under political systems that officially regard themselves as Marxist. In the poorer nations of Asia, Africa, and Latin America, Marxism remains the common philosophic denominator of many of the important social movements seeking progressive social change—both within the legitimate political processes, when permitted to do so, and outside of it, when legally suppressed. In most of the nations of Western Europe, Marxism provides the theoretical underpinnings for socialist as well as communist parties—parties that long have been incorporated into the political process, and that often have been decisive in local and national affairs. It is only in the United States that, until very recently, Marxism has remained identified exclusively with the Cold War image of the Soviet Union, and therefore dismissed out-of-hand as little more then seditious communist propaganda.

It was not until the mid-1970s that Marxism first emerged as a serious intellectual alternative to conventional social science in the United States. American Cold War thinking during the 1950s viewed Marxism as little more than an elaborate apology for Soviet Stalinism—a type of religious dogma rather than serious intellectual inquiry. Partly this was due to American parochialism, in the form of academic indifference to grand theory, combined with an enormous ignorance of Marx's actual writings. But, more significantly, it also resulted from postwar anti-communist fears, which reached their high point during the McCarthy hearings of the early 1950s. Very few identified Marxists were able to secure or retain academic positions during the ensuing decade. The most prominent sympathetic academician—C. Wright Mills, who described himself (1962) as a "plain Marxist"—never received full academic legitimacy, despite a prodigious publication record and an unquestionably significant influence on the field of sociology.

During my own undergraduate years at Columbia (1960-1964), and subsequent graduate study both at Princeton (1964-1966) and at the University of Chicago (1968-1971), Marxism was not a serious offering within general education or the social sciences. To be certain, the *Communist Manifesto* was discussed in introductory classes, occasionally sympathetically. Louis Feuer's (1959) paperback collection of edited writings from Marx and Engels was sometimes used as a text when Marx was discussed in a survey course. But, with extremely rare exceptions, no student ever read Volume I of *Capital,* Marx's single completed analysis of capitalist economic production; nor his political analyses of the mid-nineteenth-century French revolutionary currents in "The Class Struggles in France" or "The Eighteenth Brumaire of Louis Bonaparte"; nor his philosophic reflections on labor and alienation in *The Economic and Philosophical Manuscripts.* Rather, students were exposed only to the simplified analysis and polemics of the *Communist Manifesto,* which predicted the automatic movement of all societies through a fixed sequence of stages, culminating in the violent demise of capitalism and the triumph of communism. The latter was inevitably linked with the Cold War image of a totalitarian Soviet Union.

This "vulgar Marxism" could hardly be expected to appeal to predominantly middle-class academics and students, given the prevailing anticommunist ideology of the period, along with the steady postwar increase in the American middle-class standard of living. But, during the latter part of the sixties, a number of historical currents coalesced to rekindle academic interest in Marxism, particularly among graduate students and younger faculty. Central among these was the Vietnam War, which raised troubling questions concerning the relationship between economics and American foreign policy, the responsiveness, openness, and legitimacy of the federal government, and the role of militarism in American society. Of equal importance to the Vietnam War was the southern civil rights movement, which revealed an enormous discrepancy between America's egalitarian ideals and its social and political realities. The success of civil disobedience further demonstrated that unjust laws might be changed if massively disobeyed. The discovery (by social scientists) of poverty in America—first in Appalachia, then in the slums of northern cities—showed that postwar economic growth was not universally shared, a point driven home forcefully by the Johnson administration's War on Poverty, and the black urban riots of the mid-1960s. Watergate, and the resignation under fire of President Richard M. Nixon, further undermined the legitimacy of American political institutions—just as the countercultural strength and appeal of the 1960s called into question the legitimacy of social and cultural institutions.

Finally, economic growth itself slowed in the aftermath of the Vietnam War, with working-class people experiencing an actual erosion in their standard of living during the high-unemployment, high-inflation decade of the seventies.

These conditions greatly enhanced the academic appeal of Marxism in the United States, particularly to those who came of age intellectually (and politically) during the tumultuous sixties and early seventies. The prevailing social science paradigms were functionalist explanations stressing stability and societal integration, which failed to anticipate or explain the upheavals of the times. Marxism offered an alternative that claimed to account for fundamental change in both institutions and ideas. Economic stability and crisis, militarism, the legitimacy of the state, ideological beliefs—all of these were found to be encompassed within Marx's writings. Marxism therefore promised a comprehensive and systematic explanation for the turbulence of the period. It also claimed a methodological breakthrough in the study of change, in the form of *dialectical materialism*—an approach that argued that social institutions have in-built mechanisms that somehow compel change into new and higher forms.

The development of academic Marxism[1] in the United States reflected a basic cleavage within Marx's writings—one we shall document in some detail throughout this book. For many academics, the first serious examination of Marx's work focused on the so-called early writings, primarily Marx's 1844 notebooks concerning the labor process and alienation in capitalist society—a topic readily accessible to Americans since the 1963 publication (in English) of Erich Fromm's *Marx's Concept of Man.*[2] These writings revealed Marx's early concerns for the realization of human potential through satisfying, conscious, self-directed activity—a vision with obvious parallels in the counter-cultural movement of the sixties, as well as the human potential therapy movement. From these writings it was but a short step to discover an "unknown dimension"[3] of Marxist writings—a hitherto concealed, humanistic tradition that paralleled the more visible, seemingly "scientific" one that had long dominated "official" Marxism. This hidden tradition was highly critical of the dominant one, particularly its subservience to Soviet orthodoxy.

This hidden dimension was broadly termed *critical theory,* because its principal approach involved the criticism of existing social and philosophical thinking in order to reveal its often illogical and contradictory character. For fledgling Marxist academics, the discovery of this tradition typically began with largely unknown (and sometimes previously unavailable)[4] writings by Marx himself, alongside a detailed rereading of his more popular works. It then led to the ideas of the democratic socialist opposition to official Bolshevism at the time of the Soviet Revolution—the "council communists" denounced by Lenin in 1920 as "infantile."[5] One central figure was Georg Lukacs, the Hungarian communist whose 1922 essay *Reification and the Consciousness of the Proletariat* (1971b) sought to show how under capitalism one is falsely led to believe that socially constructed reality is in fact the natural order of things. In fact, following the translation of this and other key essays,[6] no one symbolized the excitement and promise of Marxism more than Lukacs, who, in a few hundred dense pages, managed to synthesize much of Western philosophy and sociology into a compelling critique of ideology that introduced the concept of *reification* (viewing an abstract concept as a real, material "thing")[7] and then showed the way to its inevitable dissolution. Equally compelling was the amalgam of psychology, cultural criticism, and philosophy found in the writings of the Frankfurt School (so-called because of its initial location in Frankfurt, Germany). This group of Marxist academics, deeply troubled by the failure of conventional Marxist theory to account for the appeal of fascism among the German lower classes during the interwar period, turned to Freudian explanations concerning the dark, irrational side of human consciousness. The first Frankfurt theorist to become widely read in the United States in the late 1960s was Herbert Marcuse, whose (1955) *Eros and Civilization*—with its emphasis on the liberating potential of humanistic love—was particularly in tune with the time.[8] Marcuse was joined by other members of the Frankfurt School— Adorno, Horkheimer, Benjamin, Bloch—and finally the prominent contemporary social philosopher, Jurgen Habermas, whose critique of the legitimating power of science struck a particularly responsive chord among a generation which had come to believe that science had run amuck in the twentieth century.

This new version of Marxism was highly complex, strongly philosophical in approach, and deeply appealing to humanistically oriented, leftist-leaning academics who had previously been exposed only to simplistic vulgarizations of Marxist theory. It seemed to promise everything: a world view that made sense of the changes undermining all facets of contemporary life; a philosophy capable of situating and criticizing the dry, irrelevant, and often mindless empiricism characteristic of much social science research; a new and complex language with which to win debating points over more conventional colleagues; and a notion of politics that contended that theory and practice were intertwined and that, therefore, academics should be politically engaged, rather than detached from the social changes of the period. A generation of progressive-minded graduate students, largely lacking in formal philosophical training, sought to become instant Marxist philosophers. In the process they frequently ignored Marx's expressed concern with developing a science, perhaps because "Marxist science" was so tainted by vulgar Marxism.

For many, however, this sojourn into Marxist philosophy proved to be disquieting. For one thing, critical theory was all too often profoundly antiempirical: It seemed to deal with abstract concepts rather than concrete institutions and actual people. Related to this was another problem: The new Marxism remained, in the last analysis, a form of philosophy, and most of those who had so recently embraced Marxism were in fact trained as empirical social scientists rather than philosophers. One possible route out of these dilemmas was found in Marx's own writings: A detailed (rather than excerpted) reading of *Capital* revealed a complex economic and social theory that dealt with the more familiar world of economic and political institutions. This theory offered an explanation of societal change that was far less mechanistic than the automatic stage theory commonly associated with Marx's work. Rather, *Capital* revealed a theory of economic instability, focusing on short- and long-term fluctuations of the business cycle, within which human activity was paramount in shaping the outcomes. There was nothing inevitable about the demise of capitalism according to this reading of Marx: Radical change required collective action, based on a correct understanding of capitalism's inherent structural weaknesses.

This was yet another Marx, whose work somehow managed to be empirical without being either empiricist or deterministic (see Chapter 3 for an elaboration of these concepts). The discovery of this version of scientific Marxism led eventually to Marxist structural theory, particularly the postwar French school dominated by the philosopher Louis

Althusser. Althusser's structuralism contained a damning condemnation of Marxist philosophy as unscientific, a criticism that rang true to many, especially those whose skills ultimately lay in the more empirically oriented social sciences rather than philosophy. This new approach was expressed in a language that, however arcane, was somehow familiar: The basic concepts seemed related to structures and functions, complex causal models with feedback loops, economic and political systems, and in general many of the conceptual markers of Parsonian systems theory, Durkheimian structural-functionalism, and pluralist political science.

Thus the 1970s witnessed a polarization of Marxist scholarship into critical philosophy on the one hand and Marxist structuralism on the other. During the 1980s, however, academic Marxism has moved in an increasingly eclectic direction. The limits of both Marxist philosophy and structuralism have led Marxist social scientists to forego purity in favor of assimilating whatever seems useful to a loosely defined Marxist framework. This is especially true within the generally pragmatic Anglo-American tradition. The most promising developments are in economic theory,[9] what is loosely termed the *theory of the state,*[10] and efforts to theorize the relationship between individual action and social structure. The latter bears brief discussion at this point, because it constitutes one of the central themes of this book.

If Marx the humanist had been concerned with overcoming alienation and exploitation through political action, then Marx the scientist had correctly recognized that such objectives required an understanding of the larger political and economic framework—particularly in its interplay with human activity. This interplay has been most frequently formulated as one of constraint.[11] In this formulation, institutions are conceived as operating according to their own internal dynamics or "logic" (Little, 1986: 29-39), which people then experience as institutional constraints on their ability freely to choose courses of action. Within such limits actors are able to exert some restricted choice, which in turn may alter the limits at some future time—although not always in ways they may desire or anticipate. The institutional dynamics so conceived are thus not quite lawlike: Unlike the natural world, the future cannot be accurately predicted (particularly in the long term) because of the often unpredictable impact of human actions on the institutional dynamic itself. In this original formulation, therefore, there remains a gap between the external institutional world and our actions: Institutions constrain us according to their own internal laws; we act as best we can; the institutions (and the laws governing them) change; we act differently as a result; and the process continues. In more recent formulations—such as Giddens's (1984) notion of structuration[12]—the process is seen as more fluid: The very dynamics of social institutions, including the limits they seem to place on our actions, are seen as constantly being modified by human activity. Humans are not seen as simply the passive bearers of social roles, but rather as active agents in accomplishing those roles—along with the institutions that comprise them.[13]

ORGANIZATION OF THIS BOOK

A number of works have appeared in recent years that address issues of Marxist methodology, particularly with reference to the status of scientific theorizing in Marx's own writings.[14] While this book shares such concerns, its overall objective is more fundamental: to understand how Marx sought to bridge the concerns of both philosophy and science in developing a theory that operates simultaneously at the levels of structure and action. In order to understand Marx's successes and failures, it is necessary to consider in some detail the specifics of his theory in its several forms: the philosophic critique of consciousness; the "scientific" analysis of capitalist economic institutions; and the historical study of politics and society. These three concerns are taken up in the three chapters that constitute the core of this volume (Part II).

First, however, it is necessary to examine the origins of Marx's thought; this we do in Part I. In the first chapter we will look at Marx's life, stressing the interplay of the historical events and intellectual currents that shaped his thinking. In so doing, we will suggest some of the key issues that Marx grappled with in developing a theory encompassing both relatively enduring social structures and those political actions capable of transforming them. In Chapter 2 we will develop these ideas further, laying out the key issues in Marxist theory. In particular, we will examine three issues I regard as central, not only to Marxist theory but to any adequate theory of social change: *determinism,* or the degree to which social structures determine human behavior; *voluntarism,* or the degree to which freely chosen actions are capable of modifying social structures; and, finally, the possible reconciliation of the two in a theory of social change. In exploring these issues, we shall also consider the relationship between *science* (as that term was understood in the nineteenth century) and philosophy in shaping Marx's thought. Chapter 3 then examines in some detail Marx's intellectual roots, focusing in particular on the philosophical legacy that shaped the debates of his time. This chapter is partly an extension of the general themes raised in the preceding one, and has the same central objectives: to show how the age-old philosophic debates over determinism and voluntarism deeply influenced Marx's thinking on the nature of science, and consequently his theory of political economy. Part II then turns to Marx's theory itself. In Chapter 4 we look at the so-called philosophical aspects of his writings, which emphasize the ways in which human actors—particularly when acting in concert with one another—are capable of shaping their historical destinies. Loosely speaking, these writings emphasize the voluntaristic aspects of his theory. As we shall see, however, Marx does not regard human agency as completely free; rather, he sees it as constrained by economic conditions, and therefore requiring an adequate understanding of those conditions if it is to be successful. Marx's own understanding is then elaborated in some detail in Chapter 5, which focuses on the operation of the capitalist economic system as he saw it. Marx's economic writings are often seen as emphasizing the deterministic aspects of social structure; in fact, as we shall see, he maintains a great deal of ambivalence (if not outright ambiguity) on this issue, particularly in *Capital*. Chapter 6 then presents Marx's analysis of politics, in the context of his concrete historical study of the relationship between politics and economics in mid-nineteenth-century Europe. It also looks at the sort of future Marx believed would result from class-based political actions grounded in an understanding of politics and economics (that is to say, grounded in his own theories).

Part III offers an attempt to reconcile some of the seemingly disparate issues raised in the preceding chapters. Chapter 7 returns to the more general concerns of Part I, focusing on the parallel questions of determinism/freedom and structure/action. The book concludes with some reflections on Marx's method, including his own understanding of the nature of science.

NOTES

1. Marxism enjoyed a significant resurgence outside the university as well, within both the social democratic left and more sectarian organizations that sought to mobilize the traditional industrial working class. The former groups tended to have an intellectual affinity for the more humanistic versions of Marxism, while the latter preferred its harder, more seemingly scientific versions. We unfortunately cannot pursue the nonacademic resurgence of Marxism in this book.

2. Fromm's book included a translation of the *Manuscripts* by Tom Bottomore.

3. This in fact was the title of an excellent collection of influential essays compiled by Howard and Klare (1972). Others, such as Gouldner (1980), have referred to the "two Marxisms."

4. In particular, these included the *Economic and Philosophical Manuscripts* (written in 1844), *The German Ideology* (1845-1846), and the *Grundrisse* (1859). See Chapters 2 and 4 for further discussion.

5. The full title of Lenin's pamphlet was *"Left-Wing" Communism: An Infantile Disorder* (1968).

6. The German translation was published in 1968; the English—under the title *History and Class Consciousness: Studies in Marxist Dialectics*—in 1971.

7. More generally, regarding humanly constructed ideas—particularly (given Marx's concerns) those concerning institutions—as naturally given. The root of *reify* is the Latin *res* (a thing, that which is real); to reify is to "make real," to mentally convert an abstract concept into a thing. Marx derived the notion of reification from Hegel. See Chapter 3.

8. As was, in an opposite sense, his much more pessimistic *One-Dimensional Man* (1964).

9. For example, Morishima (1973), Roemer (1981a, 1981b, 1982a, 1982b, 1982c, 1982d), Steedman (1977, 1981), and Wolff (1981, 1982, 1984).

10. This is concerned with the relationship between economics and politics. See, for example, Anderson (1974a, 1974b), Bloch (1966, 1967), Laclau (1977), Jessop (1982), Miliband (1969, 1977, 1982), O'Connor (1973), Offe (1984), Poulantzas (1975), and Wright (1978).

11. This was my original view (1978a, 1978b, 1979; Appelbaum and Chotiner, 1979); see also Brenner (1976), and Little (1986).

12. See Chapter 2 for further discussion.

13. We shall return to these matters in Chapter 7.

14. Particularly important among these are Cohen (1978), Keat And Urry (1975), Little (1986), McMurtry (1977), Ruben (1979), Sayer (1979), Shaw (1978), Wood (1981), and the collections of articles in Ball and Farr (1984), Mepham and Ruben (1979), and Parkinson (1982).

Acknowledgments

This book has had an uncommonly long gestation period. Its seeds were planted at the University of Chicago with the MCC and the Second Floor (West) Collective, and initially developed through a large number of formal and informal study groups at the University of California at Santa Barbara. Special long-term debts of gratitude are due to Gerald Turkel, who first introduced me to critical theory; William J. Chambliss and the participants in his *Capital* reading group; and all the members of *Das Institute*. In very different ways, James O'Connor, Jurgen Habermas, and Trent Schroyer had important initial impacts on the development of the ideas in this book. Early versions of Chapters 5 and 7 appeared in the *American Sociological Review, American Sociologist, Insurgent Sociologist,* and *Socialist Review,* and we are indebted to the editors of those journals as well as to their anonymous referees. Harry Chotiner coauthored the *Socialist Review* article that was to form the core of this book. In its present form, various drafts benefited from critical readings by Anthony Giddens, Jonathan Turner, John Foran, and William Chambliss, whose unflagging encouragement helped keep this project alive. Helpful editorial suggestions were offered by Linda Campany. Ernie Thompson's reading of the sections on Feuerbach proved invaluable, and Thomas P. Wilson's close reading of the entire manuscript was indispensable in helping me to formulate and clarify my ideas. Finally, special thanks to Art Morin and Kristin Loft-Freese for help in typing parts of the manuscript, and to Mitch Allen, Barbara Parray, and the editorial staff at Sage Publications for their suggestions.

PART I

Introduction:
The Origins of Marx's Thought

1

Marx and His Time

During a span of fewer than 35 years Marx penned sufficient materials to fill approximately 50 volumes.[1] His writings include a half dozen books published in his lifetime, with some eight additional book-length manuscripts published posthumously; countless articles that appeared in socialist journals and the popular press; numerous pamphlets and political tracts, the most famous of which is the *Communist Manifesto;* and a vast correspondence with activists and organizers, theorists, publishers, family, and, of course, Engels. This extraordinary productivity corresponded to a period of tremendous social, political, and economic change on the European continent. Marx wrote during the tumultuous middle third of the nineteenth century. His writings were shaped by the events of the period, and in turn helped to give them direction. It is important to situate his writings within this historical context, from which they are largely inseparable.

Marx was born a generation after the 1789 Revolution had overturned the old feudal order in France. The triumph of reason, trumpeted a century earlier during the Enlightenment, was embodied in the hopes and dreams of the French Revolution. The Industrial Revolution had by now spread from England to France, although Germany remained economically backward and politically disunited. The French Revolution had promised to unleash the progressive forces of science and industry from the fetters of aristocratic politics and religious dogmatism. Within four years these promises had vanished in the Reign of Terror. The ensuing experiment in democracy—the First Republic (1795-1799)—failed to stem the political and economic chaos, and led, in turn, to a constitutional monarchy under Napoleon Bonaparte. This proved to be short-lived, and in 1804 Napoleon crowned himself emperor. The brief democratic experiment had ended; order was restored, and Napoleon's armies marched through Europe, his reign ending only with his 1815 defeat at Waterloo. This in turn led to the Restoration of the French monarchy under Louis XVIII.

The first third of the nineteenth century was thus marked by a growing political conservatism, which found its parallel in the immediate philosophic precursors to Marxism (see Chapter 3). Thereafter, nine-teenth-century French history was characterized by cycles of rev-olutionary action and conservative reaction that sent waves of upheaval across the European continent (see Chapter 6). In 1830 the July Revolution forced the abdication of King Charles X, reestablishing the constitutional monarchy under Louis Philippe. The latter reigned until the agricultural and industrial recessions of 1846-1847 forced his abdication in the February 1848 Revolution. The Second Republic was then established, with Louis Napoleon Bonaparte III as its president. This, too, proved to be a brief experiment in democracy; like his uncle before him, Napoleon III soon declared himself emperor (in 1852). The Second Empire lasted until 1870, when Napoleon III was defeated during the Franco-Prussian War. With Paris under siege, the Third French Republic was declared at Versailles. By this time, however, the workers of Paris were too militant to accept the rule of the French bourgeoisie and declared their own socialist workers' republic. The Paris Commune—which was believed by Marx to embody many of the features of communist society (see Chapter 6)—lasted only a few months, until it was brutally suppressed.

These events constitute the backdrop of Marx's life and thought.[2] This intersection of biography and history (Mills, 1959) illustrates a central Marxist proposition—that the apparent separation between personal and public life is artificial and misleading. Marx's personal life was subordinated to what he regarded as his calling: to bring a scientific understanding of the dynamics of social change to the masses of industrial workers, and with it empowerment and emancipation.[3] As a 20-year-old student at the University of Berlin, Marx confidently wrote his fiancée that "with contempt, I will fling my gauntlet in the world's face and I will watch the pigmy giant crumble. . . . I will feel myself the equal of the Creator" (in Garaudy, 1967: 18). This Promethean vision sustained Marx through a lifetime of economic hardship and personal tragedy, characterized by an uncompromising commitment to research, writing, and organizing the nascent international communist movement.

ORIGINS

Following Lenin's account,[4] Marx's thought is customarily traced to three primary sources: German idealist philosophy, French socialist practice, and British economic theory (see Chapters 2 and 3 for further discussion). This simplified schema roughly corresponds both to Marx's intellectual chronology and to his geographical wanderings, and thereby serves to reinforce a widely held developmental model that I shall argue is fundamentally incorrect: that Marx began his writings as a humanistically oriented philosopher but became an increasingly hard-nosed and antihumanistic scientist as he grew older and politically wiser. In fact, I believe, Marx drew on the several sources identified by Lenin—as well as others—throughout his writing, although in different measure and with different emphasis as his theory developed. Lenin's schema diminishes the importance of numerous sources that do not fit so neatly: Spencer's and Darwin's evolutionary theories, for example, or revolutionary activity occurring among Russian peasants. Unlike many other prominent social theorists of his time, Marx never insulated himself from contrary ideas.[5] He had a voracious appetite for the printed word, once describing his favorite occupation as "bookworming" (1865, "Confessions of Marx"; in Kamenka, 1983: 53), and he learned additional languages (such as Russian) late in life in order to better follow significant political and theoretical developments.

Marx was born on May 5, 1818, in the Prussian city of Trier, which lies in the agricultural German Rhineland. Marx's father, Heinrich (born Hirschl Halevi), was a prominent attorney in a family of rabbis that included Heinrich's own father and brother, both of Trier. Marx's mother, Henriette Pressborck, was also of rabbinic parentage. Heinrich was a student of the Enlightenment who, according to one of his friends, "knew his Voltaire and his Rousseau by heart" (quoted in Garaudy, 1967: 15). The year before Marx's birth his father converted to the established Evangelical Church of Prussia in order to be able to continue in his practice of law.[6] Marx himself was baptized at age 6, which has lead a number of his biographers to attribute his frequent equation of Jewishness with money-grubbing[7] to psychological insecurity stemming from marginality.[8] Marx's father remained close to his son at least until the latter's radicalization at the University of Berlin, and he is credited with instilling in his son a lifelong love of the humanities, Enlightenment philosophy, and the classics. Marx was also strongly influenced by his next-door neighbor, Ludwig von Westphalen, a highly educated liberal humanist who was familiar with the socialist writings of Saint-Simon, and whose daughter, Jenny, Marx eventually married. Even Marx's high school principal was an advocate of political liberty and other liberal ideas (Garaudy, 1967: 15). This combination of liberal thinking and Prussian repression produced a deep disillusion-ment among the youth of Marx's generation.

God's heavenly utopia was to be replaced with a humanly created earthly one, in the form of the rationally designed society. Such ideas were especially strong in France, in the writings of Saint-Simon and Auguste Comte, as well as in the utopian teachings of Fourier. In Germany, however, economic backwardness and jurisdictional frag-mentation greatly constrained political action;[9] in this limited arena, only philosophy flourished. The German intelligentsia experienced a deep despair after Napoleon's 1815 defeat at Waterloo quashed their hopes for freedom. During the 1830s governmental repression was far-reaching: Parliament was abolished, political meetings outlawed, jury trial denied, and censorship extended to the universities. At the same time, there were hopeful signs as well: The 1832 liberal celebration at Hambach, for example, drew 25,000 demonstrators calling for German unity and constitutional government, while worker uprisings occurred in Solingen (1823), Krefeld (1828), and Aachen and Ruhrot (1830).

EARLY CONCERNS

It was against this backdrop that the young Marx entered law school at the University of Bonn in 1835. After a year of what his father derided as "wild rampaging" (quoted in Singer, 1980: 2) he transferred to the University of Berlin, where Hegel's influence remained strong.[10] Marx was soon active in a radical circle of left Hegelians who pursued truth through the "ruthless criticism of everything existing."[11] According to this neo-Hegelian tradition, the function of philosophic critique was to penetrate superficial appearances, in quest of the underlying essence or reality: for example, to reveal Christianity to be primitive mythology rather than the revealed word of God.[12] In this intellectually combative atmosphere Marx quickly abandoned law for philosophy, where his increasingly radical ideas disconcerted his father, who complained in a letter to his son that "degeneration in a learned dressing-gown with uncombed hair has replaced degeneration with a beer glass" (Singer, 1980: 2). The year before his death Heinrich wrote to his 18-year-old son the following apocryphal words:

> Your soul is obviously animated and ruled by a demon not given to all men; is this demon a heavenly or a Faustian one? Will you ever—and this is the doubt that causes me the most pain—be receptive to true human happiness, domestic happiness? Will you ever . . . be able to spread happiness to your immediate surroundings? [March 2, 1837, letter from H. Marx to K. Marx; reproduced in part in Kamenka, 1983: 10-11]

Marx's doctoral dissertation on "The Difference Between the Democritean and Epicurean Philosophy of Nature," completed at age 23, reflects his lifelong concern with the conflict between freedom and determinism,[13] his Hegelian vision of the emancipatory role of philosophy, and the importance he attached to an actively engaged (as opposed to detached) philosophical practice. In Marx's view, Epicurus had improved upon Democritus's atomism by introducing a random "swerve" into atomic movement; this, Epicurus believed, averted the complete mechanistic determinism implicit in Democritus's original theory. Marx sympathized with Epicurus's effort, if not his solution: It attempted to allow for a degree of freedom within a largely deterministic framework.[14] In this partly free, partly constrained universe, Marx regarded philosophy's role as that of *critique*—"turning itself against the exterior world" to reveal the emergent reality that is masked and distorted by surface appearances:

> As long as a single drop of blood pulses in her world-conquering and totally free heart philosophy will continually shout at her opponents the cry of Epicurus: "the profane man is not the one who destroys the gods of the multitude but the one who foists the multitudes' doctrines onto the gods. . . ." Philosophy makes no secret of it. The proclamation of Prometheus—"in a word, I detest all the Gods"—is her own profession, her own slogan against all the gods of heaven and earth who do not recognize self-consciousness as the highest divinity. [from the preface to his doctoral dissertation; in McClellan, 1977: 12-13]

In this world-transformative vision, the opposition of philosophy to action is seen to be a false one: Philosophy is engaged in the service of emancipation, although all existing philosophy will be destroyed as a result. To those who celebrate philosophy's decline, Marx offers Prometheus's response to Hermes, the messenger of the gods: "Understand this well, I would not change my evil plight for your servility" (in McClellan, 1977: 13).[15]

Marx's dissertation contains elements that I believe are retained throughout his lifetime: the notion of a structurally bounded freedom, a strong emphasis on the importance of critical thinking in demystifying false beliefs, a central role for action and change. Marx's hyperbolic writing style also reveals his sense of personal mission: I do not think it too far-fetched to argue that he identified with Prometheus, who according to classical mythology willingly suffered a painful martyrdom for his role in revealing the gods' secret of fire to humanity.

Marx's doctorate, obtained in 1841, produced no academic job offers; on the contrary, his (then) friend and mentor Bruno Bauer was fired from Bonn for his liberal beliefs. Instead, Marx was recruited by the socialist writer Moses Hess to help start a new liberal journal in Cologne, Prussia (now Germany). Within a year Marx became the editor-in-chief of the *Rheinische Zeitung*. During the next 18 months— before the journal was suppressed by Prussian authorities—he wrote articles on censorship and social philosophy, and "experienced for the first time the embarrassment of having to take part in discussions on the so-called material interests":

> The proceedings of the Rhenish Landtag [Parliament] on thefts of wood and parcelling of landed property, the official polemic which [the President] of the Rhine Province, opened against the *Rheinische Zeitung* on the conditions of the Moselle peasantry, and finally debates on free trade and protective tariffs provided the first occasions for occupying myself with economic questions. [from the autobiographical 1859 Preface to *A Critique of Political Economy;* in McClellan, 1977: 388]

In a series of critiques Marx exposed the economic interests he believed lurked beneath the surface of Parliamentary debates, arguing that the supposedly democratic governmental initiatives were in fact not helping the poor. The *Rheinische Zeitung* was criticized by radicals as well as its more moderate shareholders; when Marx attacked the Russian government of Nicolas I as reactionary the paper was shut down, enabling Marx to "withdraw from the public stage into the study" (p. 389). He married Jenny von Westphalen, to whom he had been secretly engaged for five years, and spent a brief honeymoon reading Rousseau, Montesquieu, and Hegel's *Philosophy of Right.*

If Marx's university days in Berlin were crucial in forming his philosophical framework, his subsequent period in Cologne forced him to come to grips with such concrete matters as economics and political censorship. At the end of 1843 Marx rejected a job offer in the Prussian civil service and moved to Paris. Under the tolerant July Monarchy, Paris had become a haven for socialist and anarchist radicals, who provided Marx's circle of friends and acquaintances for the next two years. Marx emerged from Paris a committed socialist revolutionary. He avidly read such theorists as Cabet, Fourier, Proudhon, Louis Blanc, Saint-Simon, and Blanqui, as well as the classical British economists. He met radical émigrés, including Bakunin, Heine, Weitling, and Ruge, along with socialist artisans and craftsmen. And he became close to Friedrich Engels, whom he had first met in Cologne. Engels, a revolutionary and a socialist, was the son of a wealthy German industrialist; he had spent his youth among his fathers' workers in the slums of the industrial Wupper Valley of the Rhine. Engels brought to Marx a concrete knowledge of life among the workers, a background in economic theory that was initially stronger than Marx's, and a lifelong commitment to support Marx's work, both intellectually and financially.

The impact of Parisian political ferment on Marx's thinking was immediate. In an 1843 article for his short-lived journal,[16] Marx already proclaimed the emerging industrial working class as the redeemer of all humanity. According to Marx, the key to German emancipation lies

in the formation of a class with radical chains . . . of a social group that is the dissolution of all social groups, of a sphere that has a universal character because of its sufferings and lays claim to no particular right because it is the object of no particular injustice but of injustice in general.

This dissolution of society, as a particular class, is the proletariat.

The proletariat is only beginning to exist in Germany through the invasion of the industrial movement. For it is not formed by the poverty produced by natural laws but by artificially induced poverty. ["Towards a Critique of Hegel's Philosophy of Right"; in McClellan, 1977: 72-73]

Marx's early discovery of the proletariat as the key to historical change provided direction for his initial attempts to rethink classical economic theory, resulting in the 1844 notes on alienation, property, communism, and philosophy first published almost a century later as the *Economic and Philosophical Manuscripts*.[17] Marx and Engels also began their writing collaboration with the publication of *The Holy Family* in 1845,[18] a characteristically scathing critique of the left Hegelian Bruno Bauer, who only a few years earlier had served as Marx's intellectual mentor. In this highly polemical work, Marx and Engels argue that the masses—rather than the "spirit of the age" (as Bauer, in Hegelian fashion, had argued)—account for progressive historical change.

CHANGING CONCERNS

In 1845 Marx was expelled from Paris by the Guizot government, moving to Brussels. He planned to write a book on economics, for which he obtained a publishers' advance; but, to the publishers' dismay, the work that was to become *Capital* would not be completed until more than two decades of additional study had passed. Instead, Marx penned the brief sketch of his emerging conception of history known as the 11 *Theses on Feuerbach*, and with Engels completed *The German Ideology*, a two-volume attack on post-Hegelian philosophy to "settle accounts with our erstwhile philosophical conscience" (Preface to *A Critique of Political Economy;* in McClellan, 1977: 390).[19] While a major part of this latter work is a tedious attack on the left Hegelian Max Stirner, *The German Ideology* remains a significant statement of Marx's solidifying ideas concerning the processes of social change.

In 1846, Marx and Engels founded the Communist Correspondence Committee, which consisted initially of German émigrés in Brussels. By this time Marx clearly identified himself as an international revolutionary with a lifetime commitment to organizing the working class, while at the same time providing it with revolutionary theory. The following year, partly at his and Engels's urging (McClellan, 1977: 221), the somewhat conspiratorial League of the Just was broadened as the International Communist League, with Marx as the president of its Brussels chapter. At the league's second London Congress, Marx and Engels were commissioned to write the statement of principles, published the following year (1848) as *The Manifesto of the Communist Party*. Partly in an effort to provide doctrinal cohesion to the league (McClellan, 1977: 195), Marx also published an attack on Proudhon's analysis of the causes of poverty.[20] In contrast to what he believed to be Proudhon's ill-founded speculations, Marx offered what he later described as the first "scientific" (if polemical) statement of his and Engels's view (from Preface to *A Critique of Political Economy;* in McClellan, 1977: 390).

In February 1848, one month after Marx and Engels completed the *Manifesto*, workers' uprisings broke out in Paris and immediately spread to Germany. For a brief period it appeared as if the proletariat might succeed in overthrowing the July Monarchy of Louis Philippe, although the French industrial and financial leadership quickly consolidated the Provisional government under its control. Marx was invited by the Provisional government to Paris even as he was being expelled from Belgium for supporting armed revolution. He soon moved back to Cologne, however, to take over the organization and editorship of a revived version of his former journal, the *Rheinische Zeitung*. Marx quickly turned the *Neue Rheinische Zeitung* into a mouthpiece for his radical ideas, publishing in turn the decree of the French National Convention sentencing Louis XVI to death, a call to left German parliamentarians to engage in extraparliamentary struggle, and a celebration of the second (June) 1848 Paris uprising as the long-awaited revolution of the proletariat against the bourgeoisie. The journal also published a series of lectures Marx had previously given under the title "Wage-Labour and Capital," which offer the first clear working-out of the economic theories that were to become fully developed in *Capital*. The *Neue Rheinische Zeitung* was accused of inciting to rebellion; Marx was expelled from Prussia for the second time, and the journal was shut down.

For a period Marx travelled in Germany, before moving briefly to Paris and then, in 1849, to London, where he would remain for the rest of his life. Marx eventually took up residence in a small two-room flat in Soho, where he set himself such tasks as reconstituting the London Communist League, organizing German workers in London, and, after obtaining a pass to the British Museum in 1851, pouring over British trade statistics and economic theory nine hours a day. The time was advantageous for study, in Marx's view, since his emerging theoretical understanding of capitalist economic cycles indicated that a growth phase had begun, dimming the prospects for the revolution that had seemed so immanent only a few years earlier. At the same time the Communist League had split over internal disputes; its headquarters were moved to Cologne, where its leaders were soon arrested and put on trial. In 1852 Marx dissolved the London branch.

Although the Marxes had always been poor, their first two decades in London were years of extreme economic privation, marked by frequent family illness that included the death of three of their six children.[21] Marx often lacked the necessary money for food, fuel, and even clothing to send his children to school. Although Marx from time to time earned modest amounts as a foreign correspondent for the liberal *New York Daily Tribune* (a position he held from 1851 to 1862), as his debts mounted family survival often depended on pawning family possessions and, occasionally, on Engels's largess. His only application for a routine job during this period—as a railway clerk—was denied on the grounds that his handwriting was illegible. Marx eventually withdrew from virtually all political activity to work full-time on his economic theory, in isolation even from the British labor movement. His life became the marginal life of the exile, a fact that some biographers believe afforded him unique insight into the workings of British society.[22] While the worst distress was temporarily alleviated when Jenny Marx inherited some money from her family estate in the mid-1850s, the Marx family did not achieve even a modest level of comfort until Marx received some inheritance funds in 1864 and the family was able to move to London's Haverstock Hills suburbs. Even then the family continued to be troubled by intermittent financial difficulties until 1868, when Engels offered to pay off Marx's debts and provide him with a modest but regular annual pension.

The letters and other reminiscences of those who were close to Marx during this period record him as a man of unyielding political conviction, an enormous capacity for work, devotion to his family, and high spirits in the face of great personal pressures. His daughter Eleanor, for example, recalled 40 years later that

> for those who knew Marx, no legend is funnier than that which portrays him as a morose, embittered, unbending and unapproachable person. . . . Such a description of the merriest, gayest person who ever lived, the man bubbling over with fun, whose laughter irresistibly won one's heart, the most friendly, gentle, and sympathetic of all companions, is a constant source of amusement to all who knew him. [in Kamenka, 1983: 48][23]

Granted that this is the nostalgic account of a devoted daughter, it is hard to deny the personal impact Marx had on his family even during their times of deepest poverty.[24] In the same account, his daughter recalled how Marx, a "unique and unrivalled story-teller" himself, also read to his small children "the whole of Homer, the *Nibelungenlied, Gadrun,* Don Quixote, The Thousand and One Nights. . . . Before I was six, I knew whole scenes from Shakespeare by heart" (in Kamenka, 1983: 50). In the cramped quarters of their two-room Soho flat there was no space for Marx to escape his family in order to work; he accommodated by writing whole chapters of the "Eighteenth Brumaire" "while acting as draughthorse for his three children who sat behind him on chairs, cracking their whips" (p. 49).

A Prussian police agent offers the following "true picture of the family life of the Communist chief, Marx" during this period (pp. 41-42):

> His large piercing fiery eyes have something demonically sinister about them. However, one can tell at the first glance that this is a man of genius and energy. His intellectual superiority exercizes an irresistable force on his surroundings. In his private life he is a highly disorderly, cynical human being and a bad manager. He lives the life of a gypsy, of an intellectual Bohemian; washing, combing, and changing his linen are things he does rarely, he likes to get drunk. He is often idle for days on

end, but when he has work to do, he will work day and night with tireless endurance. For him there is no such thing as a fixed time for waking and sleeping.

As a husband and father, Marx is the gentlest and mildest of men in spite of his wild and restless character. Marx lives in one of the worst, and therefore one of the cheapest, quarters of London. . . . There is not one clean and solid piece of furniture to be found in the whole apartment: everything is broken, tattered and torn; there is a thick coat of dust everywhere; everywhere, too, the greatest disorder. . . . None of this embarrasses Marx or his wife. You are received in the friendliest of fashions.

An 1850 letter[25] from Marx's wife, Jenny, to their friend and publisher, Joseph Weydemeyer, in which (unbeknownst to Marx) she begs for money that is owed Marx for work on a journal,[26] reveals less joyous circumstances. This letter is worth reproducing in detail not only because of the poignant account it provides of the Marx's desperate circumstances, but also because of what it reveals about working-class life in London at the time. The Marx family had just been expelled from Cologne to Paris, and then to London; in the midst of moving, their fourth child (and second son) was born. Jenny Marx laments to Weydemeyer:

You have to know London and conditions here to understand what it means to have three children and give birth to a fourth. . . . I shall describe to you just *one* day of that life, exactly as it was, and you will see that few fugitives, perhaps, have gone through anything like it. As wet-nurses here are too expensive I decided to feed my child myself in spite of terrible pains in the breast and back. But the poor little angel drank in so much anxiety and silent grief that he was already poorly and suffered horribly day and night. Since he came into the world he has not slept through a single night, but only two or three hours at the most. Recently he has had violent convulsions, too, and has been constantly at death's door [*he died six months later*]. . . . I was sitting with him like that one day when our landlady came in. We had paid her more than 250 thaler during the winter and had come to an agreement to give the money in the future not to her but to her landlord, who had a bailiff's warrant against her. She denied the agreement and demanded five pounds that we still owed her. As we did not have the money at the time . . . two bailiffs came and sequestered all my few possessions—beds, linen, clothes—everything, even my poor child's cradle and the better toys of my daughters, who stood there weeping bitterly. They threatened to take everything away in two hours. I would then have had to lie on the bare floor with my freezing children and my painful breast.

We had to leave the house the next day. It was cold, rainy and dull. My husband looked for accommodation for us. When he mentioned the four children nobody would take us in. Finally a friend helped us, we paid our rent and I hastily sold all my beds to pay the chemist, the baker, the butcher and the milkman who, alarmed by the report of the sequestration, suddenly besieged me with their bills.

Marx's principal publications during these first difficult years in London included a series of essays on the French revolutionary period 1848-1849, which appeared in a short-lived journal Marx founded in London;[27] his articles for the *Tribune;*[28] and his analysis of Louis Napoleon's 1851 coup d'etat, in which Marx provided a concrete (and rare) analysis of the relationship between class structure and state power.[29] He also studied Asiatic state systems, which were of interest to Marx because—contrary to the European experience—they exhibited strong centralized state control over production and relatively little private property.

THE ECONOMIC ANALYSIS OF CAPITALISM

In 1857 an economic crisis marked the downturn of the business cycle. Marx believed a major economic collapse to be at hand, and worked "madly through the nights" on his critique of political economy in order to stay ahead of events (letter to Engels; quoted in Singer, 1980: 7). The 800-page manuscript, which provides valuable insight into Marx's methodological thinking as well as his economic theory, was not published in Marx's lifetime and indeed was generally unavailable for almost 80 years.[30] Marx did publish a portion of this work in 1859 under the title *A Critique of Political Economy;* contrary to his hopes, it attracted no acclaim, and contains little that was not more completely addressed in *Capital* eight years later.[31] Marx thereafter continued in his economic studies. He reread Enlightenment and classical philosophy, as well as Darwin's recently published *Origin of Species,* reporting to Engels that Darwinism "provides the foundation in natural history for the theory of class struggle" (Kamenka's words, p. lxxx)[32]. His economic research focused on the history of the concept of surplus value, which Marx believed held the key to understanding the dynamics of economic production. He also studied mathematics, including integral and differential calculus. By 1863 Marx had begun the final editing of *Capital* (now subtitled *A Critique of Political Economy*); the rough draft—three volumes in length—was completed two years later, and Volume I was published to favorable reviews (Engels alone wrote seven) in 1867.[33]

With the creation of the International Working Men's Association in 1863, Marx returned to political work. The International was founded by English and French labor activists of widely divergent political persuasions, including socialists, anarchists, trade union organizers, and reform-minded social democrats. Marx, representing German artisans, was elected to the General Council, where he wrote the International's statutes, provided its inaugural address, and quickly assumed its leadership. The International held its first conference in London in 1865, with Marx giving the address to the General Council;[34] its first all-European Congress was held the following year in Geneva, with Marx attempting to exert control from London.[35] With the publication of *Capital,* Marx was able to devote the next several years to consolidating the International under the aegis of his own ideas, fighting back both anarchists and middle-class reformers. Once he was firmly and visibly at the helm, the International became a significant and widely feared force in the European labor movement, attracting even the Russian anarchist Mikhail Bakunin, whose written request for affiliation in 1868 indicated that he was proud to be Marx's disciple (Kamenka, 1983: xc).

In July 1870 Napoleon III declared war on Prussia. The subsequent French defeat two months later precipitated a political crisis in Paris, and in March 1871 the Parisian proletariat seized control for six weeks. The Paris Commune provided inspiration to the radical elements of the European labor movement. Marx himself gave several addresses to the people of Paris on behalf of the International's General Council, one of which was published, widely translated, and quickly gained Marx the public recognition (indeed, notoriety) that had thus far eluded him.[36] The Paris Commune was dominated by followers of Proudhon and other anarchists, which helped to strengthen their hand in the International, exacerbating the already worsening split engendered by Bakunin, by now no longer Marx's disciple. This rift culminated at the fifth Congress in 1872, at which Marx succeeded in maintaining control over the General Council only by transferring it to New York City, a sentence of death to which it succumbed a few years later.

During the 1870s Marx's health deteriorated. He was constantly plagued with worsening bouts of boils, headaches, gall bladder attacks, insomnia, rheumatism, and bronchitis. For long periods he was unable to work. Much of Marx's time was spent on revisions and various editions of Volume I of *Capital,* studying Russian history and language, learning about human and plant physiology, and investigating primitive landholding, especially among the Slavs. His last major writing was in 1875, an attack on the platform for a meeting in Gotha (Germany) that sought to unify various socialist factions into a single party. Marx felt that the platform was unscientific; his criticisms, which were published only posthumously by Engels in 1891,[37] lay out Marx's vision of the process by which state socialism will eventually give way to a stateless communism. In his final years, Marx was lionized, especially by Russian radicals and German Social Democrats like Bebel, Kautsky, and Bernstein.

On December 21, 1881, Marx's wife died of cancer; his daughter Jenny Longuet died in Paris two years later. Marx, whose own poor health had further deteriorated by this time, never recovered from these losses, and he died in his armchair on March 14, 1883, at age 64. After his death, Engels set about completing much of Marx's unfinished work, particularly the second and third volumes of *Capital*. In a series of writings, Engels also sought systematically to formulate Marx's methodology, something Marx himself had never done.[38] Since Engels's views were arguably more rigid than Marx's, this has resulted in considerable subsequent misunderstanding concerning Marx's method.

Marx's life reflects his commitment to fusing theory with practice, but—equally importantly—it reflects his unwillingness to pay obeisance to any system of thought in the process of developing his own ideas. Beginning with Hegel and Feuerbach and the "critical critics," Marx assimilated the ideas of others to his own emerging understanding and then moved on, often brutally deriding his former mentors. He never truly defined his own system or methodology, leaving it to others— including Engels—to define his ideas as an "ism" (in this case, historical materialism). Marx clearly believed his ideas to be grounded in ever-changing conditions that they themselves helped to create in an unending process. Marx paid homage to no one; all ideas were regarded as historically situated, to be eventually superseded by the interplay of intellectual practice and changing social, economic, and political conditions. It is therefore interesting to speculate how he would have regarded the conversion of his ideas into a frequently reified body of thought termed Marx*ism*.

Had Marx been somehow reborn into the twentieth century, I believe he would have reevaluated his nineteenth-century ideas in light of current conditions, accepting what seemed useful and acerbically critiquing the rest. He would hardly have engaged in a scholastic effort to demonstrate his loyalty to Received Doctrine—that would have been consistent with neither his method nor his personal style. What, then, would Marx have made of theorists who often seem more concerned with demonstrating the fealty of their work to Marx's writings, rather than with scientific understanding itself?

This is not a call for eclecticism: Theory does not grow by cut-and-paste methods, and Marx himself was hardly eclectic in his approach. But it is to argue strongly against the reification of social theory. It is in this spirit that we will emphasize the importance of the method of *critique* in discussing the key issues in Marxist theory in the next chapter.

NOTES

1. There is as yet no complete collection of Marx's writings. The two most comprehensive compendia are the *Marx-Engels Gesamtausgabe* (or MEGA), published in Germany and Russia over the period 1927-1935, and the 40-volume *Marx-Engels Werke,* published in Germany between 1957 and 1968. The former is both incomplete and suffers from politically motivated censorship and revision; the latter excludes early editions of major works (such as *Capital*), as well as other works. The Marx-Engels Institute in Moscow is currently supervising the publication (in English, German, and Russian) of the most complete scholarly collection to date; the first of some 50 projected volumes (in English) appeared in 1975.

2. There are a number of books that examine Marx's life, including McClellan (1975), Padover (1978), Nicolaievsky and Menchen-Helfen (1936), and Berlin (1978). There are, as can be imagined, many dozens of books on Marx's thought. I have personally found the most useful to include Avineri (1968), Meszaros (1970), Ollman (1971), Gottheil (1966), Sweezy (1942), Mandel (1968, 1970), Gouldner (1980), McClellan (1969), Tucker (1961), Cohen (1978), Zeitlin (1967), Garaudy (1967), Carver (1982), and Singer (1980). Excellent—if necessarily severely abridged—collections of Marx's writings are found in McClellan (1977) and Kamenka (1983); the latter contains particularly useful separate chronologies of Marx's life and works.

3. Or, as Marx put it in one of his earliest writings, "theory, too, will become material force once it has seized the masses" (from Introduction to the 1843-1844 *Critique of Hegel's Philosophy of Right;* in McClellan, 1977: 69).

4. "Marx is the legitimate successor of the best that was created by humanity in the nineteenth century in the shape of German philosophy, English political economy, and French socialism" (Lenin, 1971: 43).

5. Auguste Comte, the father of sociology (he coined the term), practiced what he termed "cerebral hygiene" during the writing of *Positive Polity;* he feared that contrary ideas that would distract him from the truth. With the exception of Max Weber, no nineteenth-century social theorist was as encyclopedic as Marx.

6. The Rhenish Jews had been emancipated by Napoleon; after his defeat, the Congress of Vienna assigned the region to Prussia, where Jews had no civil rights and were prohibited from the official practice of law. In 1815 Heinrich Marx appealed that the law applying to Jews be annulled, in a memorandum in which he identified with the Jewish community; his appeal was not granted by the Prussian authorities (Kamenka, 1983: xiv).

7. For example: "What is the secular basis of Judaism? Practical need, selfishness. What is the secular cult of the Jew? Haggling. What is his secular God? Money. . . . An organization of society that abolished the presupposition of haggling, and thus its possibility, would have made the Jew impossible" (from Marx's 1843 review article, "On the Jewish Question," concerning Bauer's analysis of the role of religion in dividing Christians and Jews; in McClellan, 1977: 58).

8. For example, Coser (1977: 78) writes: "Marx's lifelong aversion to the making of money is probably connected with this struggle against his Jewishness."

9. Germany had no real middle class, with industrial development just beginning in the late 1830s in the Ruhr and in Prussia. Germany itself consisted of 39 largely autonomous principalities, each with its own set of regulations, tariffs, and other restrictions on production and trade.

10. Hegel had taught at Berlin; he died five years before Marx's entry.

11. From a September 1843 letter to Arnold Ruge that was published the following year in the *Deutsch-Franzoesische Jahrbucher;* reprinted in Tucker (1972: 7-10). The full sentence reads: "But if the designing of the future and the proclamation of ready-made solutions for all time is not our affair, then we must realize all the more clearly what we have to accomplish in the present—I am speaking of a *ruthless criticism of everything existing*, ruthless in two senses: the criticism must not be afraid of its own conclusions, nor of conflict with the powers that be" (p. 8; emphasis in original). Years later Marx declared his favorite motto to be, *De Omnibus dubitandum* ["to doubt everything"] (from the 1865 "Confessions of Marx"; reproduced in Kamenka, 1983: 53).

12. In 1835 David Strauss published *The Life of Jesus,* showing the Gospels to be either inventions or primitive myths; Bruno Bauer denied Jesus existed altogether; and Ludwig Feuerbach, in 1841, argued that the *Essence of Christianity* [the title of his book] was the alienated projection of mankind's ideals and aspirations.

13. See Chapter 2 for further discussion.

14. In the fifth century B.C., the Greek philosopher Democritus had argued that reality consists only of "atoms and the void"; all existing forms of matter result from the combination and recombination of the atoms, the movements of which are completely predictable on the basis of the laws of mechanics. A century later Epicurus claimed that a subtle atomic "swerve" enabled the universe to avoid complete predictability.

15. A quarter of a century later Marx would comment that his most detested vice was servility (from the 1865 "Confessions of Marx"; reproduced in Kamenka, 1983: 53).

16. The radical *Deutsch-Franzoesische Jahrbucher,* edited by Marx and Arnold Ruge, produced only a single issue before Marx was forced by French authorities to leave Paris.

17. The *Manuscripts* were first published in MEGA in 1932; the first complete English translation was by Bottomore in 1963 (in Fromm, 1963).

18. The title refers in sarcastic fashion to the Bauer brothers. Marx and Engels also on *The* collaborated *German Ideology* and the *Communist Manifesto* (see immediately below). Engels read and commented on proofs of much of Marx's writing, and personally completed Volumes II and III of *Capital* after Marx's death.

19. Marx and Engels were never able to publish *The German Ideology,* which remained largely a work of "self-clarification," "abandoned . . . to the gnawing criticism of the mice" (Preface to *A Critique of Political Economy;* in McClellan, 1977: 390), a reference to the fact that when Marx reviewed the manuscript years later, it had been partly devoured by rats.

20. *The Poverty of Philosophy,* a characteristically ironic inversion of the title of Proudhon's book, *The Philosophy of Poverty.*

21. In 1851 Marx also had an illegitimate son, Frederick, by the family's lifelong live-in housekeeper, Helene Demuth; the child was immediately put up for adoption, and the secret made public by Engels only in 1895 on his (Engels's) death bed. (This account is, however, disputed by some; see, for example, Carver, 1981: 72-73). Marx's more critical biographers frequently imply that the deaths of his own three children were due to neglect. Thus Coser (1977: 64) writes that "three of his children died from malnutrition or lack of

proper care." In fact, two children (Guido and Franziska) died in their first year, while they were still nursing; the third, Edgar, died at age eight of "consumption." There is no evidence to suggest that the Marxes, however poor, failed adequately to care for their children. While Marx's poverty might have been a contributing factor, it should be noted that infant mortality was high among all social classes at the time. For example, although Marx himself came from a relatively well-to-do family, he was the only male (of four brothers) to survive to adulthood; of the nine children of Heinrich and Henriette Marx, five died of tuberculosis.

22. For example, Coser's (1977: 85) psychological interpretation: "His tension-ridden and conflictive private life predisposed him to see in conflict and contention the ultimate hidden motive for all history." Coser also approvingly reproduces Edmund Wilson's (1940: 316) well-known assertion that "[Marx's] trauma reflects itself in *Capital* as the trauma of mankind under industrialism; and only so sore and angry a spirit, so ill at ease in the world, could have recognized and seen into the causes of the wholesale mutilation of humanity, the grim collisions, the uncomprehended convulsions, to which the age of great profits was doomed."

23. This excerpt, originally published in 1895, refers to the period around 1858, when Eleanor Marx was about three years old.

24. In this connection it is interesting to note that his three daughters (who alone of four daughters and two sons survived to adulthood) all remained committed socialists throughout their lives. The youngest, Jenny (born 1844), married the revolutionary French journalist (and Paris Communard) Charles Longuet in 1872; the second, Laura, married the French radical socialist Paul Lafargue in 1868; and the eldest, Eleanor, became the common-law wife of Edward Aveling, a writer and publisher who translated much of Marx's work into English. Even Marx's illegitimate son Frederick became a skilled worker and active trade unionist.

25. Dated May 20; in Kamenka (1983: 33-37).

26. The money was payment for Marx's work on the *Neue Rheinische Zeitung Politisch-Okonomische Revue*; see below.

27. The journal, intended to continue the legacy of the *Neue Rheinische Zeitung,* was called the *Neue Rheinische Zeitung Politisch-Okonomische Revue;* the articles were reissued by Engels in 1895 as "The Class Struggles in France."

28. Some of these, including the 1851 series (collected and published under Marx's name in 1896 by E. M. Aveling under the title, *Revolution and Counter-Revolution in Germany*), were in fact written by Engels so Marx could devote his full attention to research.

29. First published in the New York journal *Die Revolution* under the title, "The Eighteenth Brumaire of Louis Bonaparte" (the title refers to the date of the original Napoleon's 1799 coup). Marx in 1856 also wrote an anti-Russian history (described by Kamenka, 1983: lxxviii, as "Russophobic") titled *Revelations of the Diplomatic History of the 18th Century,* published in English under the title, *The Secret Diplomatic History of the 18th Century* (London: Aveling, 1857).

30. The *Grundrisse der Kritik der Politischen Okonomie* [Foundations for A Critique of Political Economy] was published in Moscow in 1939-1941. A segment was translated into English in 1964 under the title *Precapitalist Economic Formations;* a complete version was published in English by Martin Nicolaus in 1973 under the title *Grundrisse.*

31. The preface does contain a brief autobiographical intellectual sketch, however, which I have frequently cited in this chapter; it also contains a famous—and extremely deterministic—simplified summary of Marx's theory that is unfortunately frequently quoted as definitive.

32. Marx admired Darwin's theory; he sent copies of the second edition of *Capital* to Darwin and Spencer, and Engels's eulogy at Marx's grave claimed that "just as Darwin discovered the law of development of organic nature, so Marx discovered the law of development of human history." Marx also spent much of 1860 responding to a brochure by a left-wing geologist named Karl Vogt accusing Marx of blackmail and forgery (*Herr Vogt,* London, 1860), and attempting to sue newspapers for defamation over the matter.

33. Volume I of *Capital* went through four editions (1867, 1872, 1883, and 1890), reflecting Marx's changing thinking and Engels's editing. It was soon published in Russian (1872), French (1872-1875), Italian (1886), and English (1887). The three-volume English set, currently most widely in use, reflects the original English edition of 1887, edited by Engels; it was published in the United States on the 1967 centenary of the original *Capital* (1867) by International Publishers. Volumes II and III were never finished by Marx, but Engels produced edited versions that appeared in 1885 (Volume II) and 1884 (Volume III). The extensive materials on surplus value were deleted by Marx from the original draft versions of *Capital;* they are currently available, in English, in a three-volume set entitled *Theories of Surplus Value* (1963, 1968, 1971).

34. Published in 1898 under the title, *Value, Price, and Profit* (London: Aveling).

35. For financial reasons, Marx was able personally to attend only the fifth and final Congress of the International.

36. The address was known under the title, "The Civil War in France." Marx was popularly believed personally to have directed the uprising (a charge he truthfully and publicly denied), which reinforced fears of a worldwide communist conspiracy with Marx at the helm (Singer, 1980: 8; Kamenka, 1983: xciv).

37. The English translation, under the title *Critique of the Gotha Program,* first appeared in 1933. Marx also wrote a chapter ("Aus der 'Kritischen Geschichte'"; Chapter 10) for Engels's book *Anti-Duhring* in 1877, and an article for the French *Revue Socialiste* ('Enquete ouvriere') in 1880. A letter of March 8, 1881, to the Russian socialist Vera Zasulich (reprinted in McClellan, 1977: 576-580) is also of interest because of its seemingly heretical (if prophetic) contention that Russian agriculture might in fact bypass a capitalist phase on its eventual way to communism (see Chapter 5).

38. For example, in *Anti-Duhring* (1939) and *Dialectics of Nature* (translated 1954), and his September 21, 1890, letter to J. Bloch.

2

Key Issues in Marxist Theory

In reading classical political economy through the lens of critical theory,[1] Marx sought to reconcile two seemingly antithetical nineteenth-century intellectual traditions, science (as then understood) and critical philosophy. An appreciation of the significance of this effort is central to understanding Marx's strengths and weaknesses. That Marx did not entirely succeed is not surprising: No one has, and only in the past decade has this effort again been joined in the social sciences in a way that portends possible advance.

The remainder of this book will trace Marx's intellectual route, and hopefully thereby point the way toward a resolution of some of the central conceptual dilemmas he addressed. Before proceeding, however, it will be useful to lay out those dilemmas clearly. We shall do so at this point under the general headings of science, philosophy, and praxis.

Science and Determinism

As the natural sciences proved increasingly successful in explaining physical, chemical, and biological phenomena during the eighteenth and nineteenth centuries, their general approach came to be regarded as appropriate for the emerging social sciences as well. That approach came to be labeled *positivism*, a term coined by Auguste Comte, a nineteenth-century French thinker regarded as the founder of sociology. In Comte's usage, *positivism* was a polemical term indicating the transition from metaphysical philosophy to science (Marcuse, 1969: 340-341); it celebrated the "positivity" of facts—the possibility of obtaining truthful knowledge from unbiased observation guided by theory. Since the term *positivism* has come to have a number of different and often contradictory meanings, I shall use a related term to denote the particular view of science that dominated Marx's time and his thinking: the *natural science model.* It is important to note from the outset that most philosophers of science no longer regard the model I shall describe below as adequately capturing the scientific method. Moreover, there is considerable disagreement over the extent to which the assumptions and methods of natural science, however conceived, are applicable to social phenomena at all. While these issues will be touched upon throughout the remainder of this book, for the present let me simply note that at the time Marx was writing it was widely accepted that the natural science model presented below described the practice of scientists, and provided the correct model for social scientists as well.

Let us first briefly consider the theory of knowledge (or *epistemology*) implicit in the natural science model. According to this model, objective knowledge—"scientific truth"—is possible on the basis of inferences drawn from unbiased observations.[2] Such knowledge is to be free from all prior conceptions and theorizing: "The facts" should be allowed to "speak for themselves." This theory of knowledge is rooted in the empiricist epistemologies of Locke and Hume from the eighteenth century (see Chapter 3). The natural science model further assumes that its version of science alone provides the road to factual truth. All other forms of human understanding—intuition, poetry, religious beliefs, other forms of personal awareness—are inferior sources of factual knowledge, whatever value they may have in their proper domains. Knowledge obtained by nonscientific means is thus to be scorned. There is an abiding optimism that science will some day free humanity from all dogma and superstition. In the process, it will compel nature—and society—to disclose their innermost secrets. The practical result will be the subjugation of both the natural and social worlds to human dominion, which in turn will pave the way for a socially engineered earthly utopia—a perfect society in a perfectly humanized nature.

This epistemology is linked to a corresponding notion of the nature of reality (or *ontology*), one that continues a long-standing Western intellectual legacy. That legacy was born with the Greek philosopher Democritus in the fourth and fifth centuries B.C., and, after lying dormant for over a thousand years, was revived with Bacon and the scientific revolution in the seventeenth century. This ontology is termed *materialism,* in that it emphasizes the primacy of the material world as the fundamental building block of reality. *Material* may be understood in physical terms (Democritus's atoms) or in more sociological ones (Durkheim's "social facts"), but the central point is that the material world is conceived of as external to—and independent of—human perception and consciousness. The material world—reality—is prior to all understanding.

Furthermore, the material world is so organized as to be entirely predictable, at least in principle: It is conceived as a vast machine whose interconnections, once properly mapped, permit the scientifically trained expert accurately to predict the future entirely on the basis of the present. The natural science model thus holds nature to be fully deterministic: The present determines the future, and given a full knowledge of initial conditions—along with an adequate theory about their interrelations—future events can in principle be predicted. The task of scientific theory is thus to generate universally applicable laws that permit such prediction, and thereby afford some degree of control over the future. In the view of the seventeenth-century philosopher Sir Francis Bacon, "we command nature by obeying her" (Leiss, 1974: 58).[3] Prediction implies power, and the potentially highly accurate predictions of science portend significant power—a feature that was attractive to Marx, whose primary concern was empowering the working class to alter fundamentally the existing social order.

The French enlightenment *philosophes,* notably Turgot and Condorcet, extended the materialism of natural science to the social world, and eventually gave birth to sociology. Saint-Simon, Comte, and Durkheim all placed their hopes on a social science that could reproduce the apparent successes of mathematics and physics in the domain of sociology. In their view, the natural science model was to be extended—unchanged—to the study of social phenomena. Stated somewhat differently, the social sciences could hope only to achieve success if they faithfully copied the methodology implicit in the natural science model.

Marx unquestionably adhered to the natural science model as depicted above. He sought to understand the laws of capitalist economic production, in order to place this understanding in the service of the working class so that they might realize a better future. He frequently spoke in the language of an objective, deterministic science, particularly when referring to the "inevitable" demise of capitalism. It is therefore easy to read Marx as an unyielding proponent of the natural science model, since a large part of his methodological self-understanding was framed in the scientific spirit of his times. But this is only half the story, since Marx could never accept a strictly deterministic version of science that—pushed to its logical limits—left no room for freely chosen, conscious human activity. In his celebrated phrase (*Eighteenth Brumaire;* in McClellan, 1977: 300),

> Men make their own history, but they do not make it just as they please;
> they do not make it under circumstances chosen by themselves, but under
> circumstances directly encountered, given, and transmitted from the past.

This single sentence contains the paradoxical formulation that constitutes one of Marx's most important contributions to social science: an orientation that seeks to treat human beings both as shaped by social forces and as shaper of those forces, the objects as well as the subjects of history (Lukacs, 1971b). If the second clause in the above phrase reflects Marx's concern with developing a scientific theory of social change, the first constitutes his mandate to revolutionary socialism: to understand how people can break through their mental blinders and institutional barriers in order to remake consciously a world that enables them to realize their fullest potential. This linking of external freedom with free, conscious mental activity is a legacy of the second nineteenth-century intellectual tradition that influenced Marx—critical philosophy.

Idealist Philosophy and Freedom

It would seem that science, at least as construed by the natural science model of the nineteenth century, allows little latitude for human choice. Freedom, in this view, is necessarily limited: It is restricted to the ability impartially to chart the laws that govern the world, and then to behave according to those laws. The laws of ballistics can never be changed, but if one understands them one can send a missile halfway around the world with unerring accuracy. Such freedom is not really freedom, of course, for everything in the universe—including human behavior and even knowledge—is ultimately determined by the forces operating in a lawful world. In this formulation, a deterministic science is counterposed to a "voluntaristic" metaphysics or philosophy.

Voluntarism—the belief that voluntary choice or will can govern human action—reflects the assumption that our human ability to think exempts us from the determinism that seemingly governs the natural world. According to this view, humans—unlike animals—are not condemned blindly to respond to external stimuli. Rather, we can think about the forces that act upon us, mentally generate options, and then choose among alternative courses of action. Freedom in this sense stems from the self-evident fact that we seem to have far more control over what goes on inside our minds than we do over the external world.

The term *reason* is frequently used by philosophers to refer to the ability of the human mind to apprehend directly or intuitively truthful or correct principles without the need for direct observation or other forms of sensory input. *Rationalism* refers to the belief that reason by itself is capable of providing truthful knowledge, in contrast to the empiricist epistemology that underlies the natural science model, namely, the belief that truth originates in experience alone (see Chapter 3). Plato believed humans were rational in this sense: He held knowledge resulted from careful, logical thought, which reveals universal truths present in all human minds. Truth, Plato surmised, can be achieved through dialogue, which, employing the faculty of reason, strips away all falsehood. Plato believed that such knowledge was ultimately superior to observation, since the latter—no matter how seemingly unbiased—was necessarily subject to all manner of perceptual delusion.

This rationalist epistemology has a corresponding ontology: the view that reality consists of mental ideas rather than external facts. This position is often termed *philosophical idealism,* since it stresses the ontological primacy of the idea or concept. Even prior to Plato, the Greek philosopher-mathematician Pythagoras had argued that reality was a cosmos—an orderly, harmonious system revealed in the beautiful symmetries of mathematics. Plato, of course, believed that the cosmos actually consisted of pure mathematical forms, of which the physical forms of the external world were simply imperfect representations. Reason alone, according to Plato, could apprehend these changeless forms; classical epistemology in general was greatly concerned to explain the seeming correspondence between the cosmos and the internal logic of the mind.

In modern times few philosophers adhere to strictly idealist ontologies; rationalist (or at least partly rationalist) epistemologies, on the other hand, continue to be influential. At the turn of the eighteenth and nineteenth centuries, Marx's own thinking was strongly influenced by Hegelian idealism, which in turn grew out of the idealism implicit in Kant's epistemology, which looked to the mind as a principal source of truth. We shall examine the idealist roots of Marx's thought in Chapter 3, and particularly Hegel's reformulation of Kant. Hegel's approach significantly shaped Marx's thinking: Both were concerned with freedom, and both believed that freedom in the external world presupposes freedom in thought. One of the key barriers to effective human action and social change, according to both Hegel and Marx, is reification (see Preface, note 7). Marx argued that massive reification characterized both everyday beliefs, as when workers view inequality as part of the natural (and therefore unavoidable) order of nature, and social theories, as when economists confuse their historically situated theoretical constructs with reality itself. One of the key tasks of knowledge, in Marx's view, is therefore to break through the "veil of reification" (Lukacs, 1971b: 86), so that people can rationally act to change the world. Without this step, our theories will be incorrect, our actions ill-informed and therefore doomed to failure. Such concerns led Marx to spend a considerable part of his time attacking ideologies, erroneous belief systems that serve to perpetuate the status quo.

For Marx, revolution was not a mechanical activity of spelling out in accurate detail the complex of forces operating at a given moment, and then sitting back and waiting for history to "take its course." While revolutionary struggle requires a clear understanding of the social forces operating to produce social change, it also involves continual choices and an openness to the moment—it involves freedom as well as necessity. If social science enables us to understand the operation of social forces, philosophy provides the emphasis on cognitive emancipation through reason. Marx spent his early years studying philosophy. It heavily influenced his initial writing, and provided him with concerns that recur throughout his work.

As noted earlier, Marx's idealist philosophical legacy would appear antithetical to his naturalistically expressed scientific concerns. We have seen that idealist philosophy looks for truth within the internal realm of mind or consciousness, while natural science seeks it in the external world of observable material things. As Marx himself notes in his 1859 Preface to *A Critique of Political Economy* (in McClellan, 1977: 389-390),

A distinction should always be made between the material transformation of the economic conditions of production, which can be determined with the precision of natural science, and the legal, religious, aesthetic, or philosophic—in short, ideological forms in which men become conscious of this conflict and fight it out.

Idealist philosophy emphasizes freedom and choice; science stresses determinism and predictability. The one looks for truth in the rational processes of the subjective mind; the other seeks objectivity by being empirically grounded and—in its empiricist variant—denies the role of the mind as an independent source of truth. Reconciling these two traditions has proven to be an intractable problem, a fact that accounts for much of the ambiguity and confusion we will encounter in Marx's writing. Marx's attempt at synthesis produced a breakthrough in the understanding of the role of human agency in history. To appreciate fully this contribution, it is necessary to consider Marx's conceptualization of human activity—the notion of *praxis*.

Praxis and Structuration

In 1845 the young Marx (he was then 27) jotted down 11 notes to serve as an outline for his changing thinking on philosophy and science.

It is during this time that Marx moved away from purely abstract philosophical critique toward a more scientific perspective (see next chapter). The notes are primarily concerned with the ideas of the German philosopher Ludwig Feuerbach, who was attempting to "invert" Hegel's idealist philosophy by grounding it in concrete, sensory human experience. Marx's first *Thesis on Feuerbach* is of particular interest. In that thesis, Marx (in McClellan, 1977: 156) comments:

> The chief defect of all hitherto existing materialism (that of Feuerbach included) is that the thing, reality, sensuousness, is conceived only in the form of the object or of contemplation, but not as sensuous human activity, practice, not subjectively. Hence in contradistinction to materialism, the active side was developed abstractly by idealism—which, of course, does not know actual, sensuous activity as such.

In this passage Marx unfavorably compares the passivity of materialism with the "active side" of philosophy; at the same time he criticizes the latter for its abstractness. Materialism studies the real and concrete, but in a passive way; philosophy stresses human activity, yet remains purely speculative. To these Marx counterposes "sensuous human activity"—a category that combines both the concrete and the active. Marx's term for such activity is *praxis*.

The classical notion of praxis refers to freely chosen, conscious activity—in other words, informed action. In Aristotle's original formulation, praxis was distinguished from *theoria:* The latter is knowledge for its own sake, while the former is "practical" in that it is oriented toward (and informed by) civic life in the political community. Marx, drawing on Aristotle, similarly regards praxis as the synthesis of theory and practice: Praxis is theoretically informed action, in which the latter feeds back on and modifies the former in an ongoing process.[4]

Although he often characterizes his approach in the language of the natural science model, Marx's historical and theoretical writings in fact reflect a blending of science and philosophy in the spirit of the first Thesis. While I will develop this argument at length throughout the book, it is useful to bear in mind at least two senses in which Marx does so: in the role accorded praxis in ordinary human activity, and in his treatment of science as a form of praxis.

Early in Marx's writings, the labor process is offered as a paradigm instance of praxis. Borrowing from Hegel, Marx characterizes human labor as the mutual transformation of the material world and humankind (*Capital,* Volume I, 1867: part III, Chapter VII, section 1, p. 177):[5]

> Labour is, in the first place, a process in which both man and Nature participate, and in which man of his own accord starts, regulates, and

controls the material re-actions between himself and Nature. He opposes himself to Nature as one of her own forces, set in motion arms and legs, head and hands, and the natural forces of his body, in order to appropriate Nature's productions in a form adapted to his own wants. By thus acting on the external world and changing it, he at the same time changes his own nature. He develops his slumbering powers and compels them to act in obedience to his sway.

Humans are not condemned to respond passively and adapt to an externally changing environment; rather, they are capable of remaking their world according to their own ideas and plans. A well-known example from Engels (1968),[6] familiar to Marx, will serve to illustrate this point. We are not concerned with the historical accuracy of this example, which was based on the limited evidence available to Engels at the time, but use it only to reveal Marx's ways of thinking about the mutual transformation of humanity/nature.

Early hunters and gatherers, according to Engels, were organized socially into small communal (classless) groups, the outlooks of which stressed cooperation and altruism. But this was not a static situation. Such primitive subsistence techniques left these groups at the mercy of frequently harsh and unpredictable natural conditions. One possible solution to the perennial potential problem of scarcity was to generate a stable food supply through crop cultivation and animal husbandry. Such planned inventions resulted in new and unanticipated social forms: settled agricultural communities, surplus production, and the possible emergence of social classes. When class-based social relations finally did emerge, the prevailing ways of thinking changed accordingly: Altruism and cooperation gave way to selfishness and competition. New institutions arose, with new ways of thinking; these in turn gave rise to new forms of labor, which further altered the external environment and thereby the individuals, their society, and their consciousness.

In this simplified example we see a form of historical praxis: Theory and practice modify one another in an ongoing dialectic. Furthermore, although human actors consciously seek to shape their world, in so doing they create results they neither anticipate nor desire. The contemporary British sociologist Anthony Giddens (1979, 1981, 1984) has termed this dynamic *structuration*—the process whereby our everyday actions are structured by antecedent conditions, conditions that are then both reproduced and modified as we act to produce other structuring conditions. Social structures, in this view, thus operate in a twofold fashion, reflecting what Giddens terms the *duality of structure*: They are both a resource for, as well as an outcome of, our actions. Social structures simultaneously constrain and enable. Insofar as we fail adequately to understand the relationship between preexisting structure and action, the results will be unintended, the process outside our control. Praxis, in this sense, is open-ended: It leads to unanticipated consequences.

While all informed human activity thus entails praxis, routine activity is not based on systematic knowledge and is therefore an inferior form of praxis. Daily actions are typically guided by incorrect beliefs, poor theories, and faulty information, resulting in unexpected and undesired results. According to Marx, there is one form of action that potentially provides sufficient understanding to avoid such unexpected outcomes: action that is informed by a scientifically correct theory. An adequate scientific understanding of social and economic forces therefore permits humankind effectively to control its destiny. Marx clearly believed his own theories would fulfill this role.

Conclusion: Marxism and Science

Marx's writings operate simultaneously on two levels. On the one hand, they continually seek to demystify the false knowledge that obscures our understanding of events while giving us the illusion that we are somehow in control. Such beliefs range from simple, everyday notions to complex ideologies—belief systems that, in Marx's view, enable the dominant class to control the thinking of those who are subordinate. For Marx, the emerging science of political economy was in fact ideological in this sense, and Marx's writings devote considerable attention to debunking its prevailing notions. On the second level, therefore, Marx seeks to develop his own *scientific theory* as a guide to truly effective action. Such theory must reflect the dual role of structure, and its methodology must permit its central concepts to be themselves transformed in light of praxis.

As we shall see in the next chapter, Marx saw himself as developing a scientific alternative to three traditions that dominated the philosophical and political discourse of his time—speculative philosophy, utopian programmatics, and pseudo-scientific economics.[7] Concerning the first, idealist philosophers such as Hegel had long sought to demonstrate that the movement of history could be understood in terms of the development of ideas. Marx countered that refuting an idea, by itself, had little impact on the socioeconomic system in which it originated. What was needed instead was an adequate understanding of the mechanisms that governed the operation of the social order—an understanding to be sought in the natural science model. Concerning the second tradition, Marx argued that the utopian socialists of his time were full of visionary ideas about the sort of society they wished to create, but they, too, lacked any understanding of the concrete mechanisms by which the old order might give birth to the new. Again, Marx turned to the natural science model for guidance. Finally, concerning the third tradition, political economy claimed to offer just such an understanding; it purported to have adapted the methods of natural science to the study of the economy. In this case, however, the results were misleading, for in Marx's view political economy was full of ideological distortions and therefore far from scientific. We shall explore the reasons for this in Chapter 5, but one key criticism can be noted at this time: Political economy falsely regarded the apparent laws of capitalism as universal features of all societies.

Marx sought to fight these various heresies with the club of science. Not only did this cloak his efforts in the mantle of scientific prestige, thereby hopefully silencing his opponents, but it also promised success in his quest to understand and transform the capitalist system. Marx unquestionably believed in the ability of the natural science model to explain both the natural and the social worlds. The great debates over the relevance of natural science methods for social phenomena did not occur during Marx's lifetime; the natural science model itself did not come under sustained and telling attack until the 1950s (see, e.g., Suppe, 1974: 125-191). It was not until the 1962 publication of Thomas Kuhn's (1970) *Structure of Scientific Revolutions* that it became generally accepted (at least among philosophers of science) that the empiricist assumptions underlying the natural science model were in fact not tenable in the domain of physics, much less sociology. So perhaps Marx is not to be faulted for often speaking as if he were creating a social physics (or biology, his preferred analogy). As we shall see in Part II of this book, his methodological self-understanding was strongly tempered by his philosophical legacy, which prevented him in practice from developing the kind of science he presumably espoused. In fact, Marx remains exciting precisely because he managed to straddle—however uncomfortably at times—the interrelated gulfs between philosophy and science, agency and structure, human freedom and social determinism.

Marx's strengths and weaknesses must be evaluated in light of these circumstances. It is my belief that his methodological self-understanding was farsighted in light of his contemporaneous intellectual traditions, but that it has largely heuristic value as a guide to discussion today. Marx's notions of science are both limited and ambiguous, and must be interpreted in light of more contemporary understanding. There is no denying that Marx's vision was limited by the philosophical debates of his time, and that considerable subsequent advances have been made in the philosophy of science. Similarly, the substantive content of his theories must be judged in their historical context. We shall find those theories to be remarkably prescient for their time, but historically situated nevertheless.

NOTES

1. The classical British economists and German idealist philosophy both had enormous influence on Marx, as we shall see in the next chapter.

2. This view was formally developed by the Vienna Circle of Logical Positivism during the first quarter of this century. For a detailed historical discussion and analysis, see Suppe (1974: 6-56).

3. In Bacon's suggestive sexual imagery, "For you but have to follow and as it were hound nature in her wanderings, and you will be able, when you like, to lead and drive her afterwards to the same place again" (from *The Advancement of Learning: Works IV;* quoted in Leiss, 1974: 59).

4. In the classical Greek tradition, civic life was the highest form of praxis (Bernstein, 1971: ix-xi). For Marx, praxis is similarly directed at full participation in the political community. Since such participation is denied the dominated classes in class-based societies, praxis necessarily entails action aimed at empowering the underclass through altering class relations—in Marx's terms, *class struggle.* Class struggle is thus a form of praxis, informed by (and modifying) social theory in a mutually constitutive dialectic.

5. For an extended analysis of this point, see Marcuse (1969: 73-80); also, Marx's critique of Hegel in his 1844 *Economic and Philosophical Manuscripts* (in McClellan, 1977: 101).

6. From Engels's 1884 *Origin of the Family, Private Property, and the State.*

7. I am indebted to Thomas P. Wilson for his helpful clarifications on this point.

3

The Origins of Marxist Theory

Dualistic thinking is as old as thought itself. Human beings exist in a material world and, like all things, are subject to its laws. Yet at the same time, the ability to reason seems to afford some degree of freedom from a strict determinism. The very use of language would seem to entail a fundamental split between *I* and *it*, subject and object, the mental and the material: The utterance of the pronoun *I* implies the existence of a freely acting subject and an acted-upon predicate.

In the West, the emergence of philosophy in classical times seriously questioned the identity between experience and concept. The task of philosophy, as Radin (1957: 248) put it, "is always the same—an original, moving, shapeless or undifferentiated world must be brought to rest and given stable form." For philosophy's task to be realized, the chaotic and unpredictable world of Homer's *Iliad*—in which capricious gods play havoc with the plans of humans—must yield to one that is guided by highly abstract, binding laws that are somehow understood by the human mind.

Classical Roots of Marxist Theory

The earliest Greek philosophers distinguished *logos,* the rational principle they believed governed the universe, from *doxa,* practical or everyday experience. Doxa is the realm of ever-changing sense-experience; logos is constant and immutable. Theory[1]—philosophy—entails the contemplation of the logos that underlies doxa. It penetrates and questions the "natural attitude" (Shutz, 1970: 72-73) of our everyday thinking, thereby undermining the naive identification of perceived reality with reality itself. Classical philosophy argued that *appearance* and *reality* are not the same: The latter is mediated by perception to produce the former.

Although the world within which we act and think often appears to be so real as to remain largely unquestioned, underlying experienced reality is yet another level that is in fact "really" real—a world whose processes and relations are hidden and must be sought out. Such an underlying core governs the surface world, shaping its development, containing its future possibilities. It has been apparent to most people throughout history, for example, that the moon and sun somehow revolve around the earth; yet underlying this misleading appearance lies a complex set of relationships that, when understood, reveals a truth that is very different. Dogmatic belief in the reality of an earth-centered universe long inhibited the development of science and technology. If knowledge is to advance, the identity between surface appearance and underlying reality must be broken.

Classical Idealism

Efforts to distinguish logos from doxa in western philosophy began in the seventh century B.C.,[2] with the first significant contributions being made a century later by the Greek mathematician Pythagoras. Pythagoras believed the universe to be an orderly *cosmos* whose essentially harmonious nature was at root mathematical, with numerical relations underlying the seeming disparity of sense-experience.[3] In Pythagoras's cosmology, various combinations of odd and even numbers were held to produce various geometric forms; these, in turn, were seen as giving rise to such physical substances as fire and air. Pythagoras's legacy—largely through Plato, whom he strongly influenced—was the belief in a nonmaterial cosmos accessible to reason alone, the discovery of which proceeds independently of empirical study. Mathematical truths are derived deductively, on the basis of logical inference from self-evident assumptions and propositions. The results of such purely mental activity are then found to correspond to the empirical world. The road to understanding reality, in this formulation, is found in the mind, not in sense-based experience, which is regarded as an imperfect, evanescent copy.

During the fourth and fifth centuries B.C., Plato (our source for Socrates's teachings) sought to demonstrate that purely mental knowledge was in fact more real than knowledge deriving from observation or other sensory origins. Behind physical objects, which are situated in time and space, lies the atemporal, aspatial world of the *ideai*—of thoughts or *forms* (as the original Greek term is usually translated). These forms enjoy an existence independent of the flux of the material world.[4] They are accessible to reason rather than perception, since it is through reason alone we arrive at the reality that underlies the perceptual world. This reality of the forms is eternal: It changes neither in time nor space, because it is outside of both. Reality is inter-subjectively shared at the level of the concept, and not, as one might believe, perception. While individual perceptions may vary (and therefore lead us into error), concepts are universal and can be established as such through discourse. This, of course, was the intent of the Socratic dialogue—to rationally deduce universal truths through logical discussions that strip away all error. As Plato states in the *Timaeus,*

> That which is apprehended by intelligence and reason is always in the same state; but that which is conceived by opinion with the help of sensations and without reason, is always in a process of becoming and perishing and never really is. [Plato, 1949: 11-12]

Any theory of knowledge must offer an account of the correspondence between the world outside the mind and the mental representations of that world. Plato, for example, believed that all mental concepts could ultimately be decomposed into two irreducible triangles (the half-square and half-equilateral), which were "reflected in space" as four basic geometrical forms—which in turn combined to produce the multiplicity of concepts representing the diversity of external experience. However dubious this cosmology, Plato's legacy for idealist philosophy has unquestionably been substantial: the rationalist belief that truth can be obtained through purely mental activity.

Classical Materialism

The effort to distinguish logos from doxa does not necessarily lead to philosophic idealism, however. Scientific materialism is similarly motivated by the desire to make order out of chaos—to reduce the "many" of experience to a reduced number of elements governed by a relatively small set of lawful (i.e., recurrent) interrelationships. We readily recognize the success of such an effort in chemistry and physics, in which—for example—the periodic table reduces the countless forms of matter to a hundred or so constituent elements and further prescribes their possible combinations.

The human quest for such definition and order is probably as old as language. In Western culture the first systematic efforts to develop a materialist explanation in this direction are found in preclassical cosmology—for example, the efforts of the seventh-century B.C. philosopher Thales to reduce all matter to a single element (water), or of the pluralists in the sixth century to account for matter in terms of primary "roots."[5] The atomic theory of matter is usually credited to the fifth-century philosopher Leucippus, whose pupil—Democritus— expanded upon (and committed to writing) the views of his mentor. In a formulation similar in some respects to contemporary atomic theory, Democritus sought to explain qualitative differences in quantitative terms, according to which reality consists of nothing more than "atoms and the void"[6]—identical, homogeneous primary particles combining and recombining in empty space to create the manifold of experienced reality.

The relationship among the atoms, according to Democritus, is *mechanistic*—that is, one of cause-and-effect, whereby one atom transmits momentum to another through direct impact. These impacts are *deterministic* in that, given sufficient information concerning the mass, location, and movement of each atom, one could in theory predict all future states of the system, as each set of impacts give rise to predictable motions and future impacts. Such a formulation would appear to rule out the possibility of human agency in shaping the world. We have already commented (Chapter 1) on Marx's rejection of Democritus's rigid determinism on these grounds, in favor of Epicurus's presumably less deterministic random "swerve." It is significant that Marx's first major philosophic work was concerned with mechanistic materialism; although he later sought to develop a dialectical alternative to a strict materialism, his early concerns with predictability and causation were never abandoned. Nor, as we shall see, were they ever entirely reconciled with his equally strong desire to insert human agency into social history.

Although Democritus's materialism can be seen as a precursor of early twentieth-century atomic theory, his methodology remained purely speculative: Democritus gathered no data to test his assertions. Greek atomism—like the Greek idealism of Pythagoras or Plato— remained resolutely antiempirical. The classical period ended with the triumph of Aristotelian science, however, which—unlike the phi- losophies of Democritus and Plato—emphasized the importance of observation. Observation was not a source of systematic hypothesis- testing for Aristotle, however; rather, it was used to confirm prior notions on the basis of largely impressionistic data. Furthermore, Aristotle adhered to a belief in *telos*—indwelling purposes that govern the behavior and future development of bodies. With the fall of Rome in the fifth century, Greek science was largely lost for some seven hundred years, although aspects survived in the medieval church. Mechanistic theories did not fully reemerge until the mid-sixteenth century, partly because of the increasing importance of machines at that time (for example, Leonardo da Vinci's sketches of flying machines), and partly because of the appearance of Latin translations of the writings of the classical mechanistic theorist Archimedes. But the main reason for the revival of mechanism in philosophy was the resounding triumph of mechanistic theories within science itself.

The Scientific Revolution
and Empiricist Philosophy

Galileo's (1564-1642) contributions to dynamics provided mechanistic theories with their modern foundation. Contrary to the classical position inherited from Aristotle, Galileo rejected the notion that bodies possess inherent qualities that somehow determine their motion. Rather, building on the theories of Kepler, he argued that bodies are inert—that is, a body at rest will tend to remain at rest, while a body in motion will tend to remain in motion. In other words, bodies tend to retain their current state; an *external* force is required for change to occur. All purposiveness is absent from the mechanistic universe: Future states of matter are entirely explained by forces present in the current state. Galileo preoccupied himself with deriving laws of motion on the basis of mechanistic principles, according to which the movements of falling bodies, rolling balls, and conical pendulums were all predictable.

Unlike his classical predecessors, Galileo sought to test his theories through observation by means of the controlled experiment, governed by laws that expressed physical regularities. Galileo stated the laws that expressed physical regularities in mathematical terms; this, in turn, required that the phenomena in question be quantified in order for the laws to be tested. This approach permitted Galileo to move back and forth between mathematical manipulation of concepts and the physical data necessary for testing those concepts. This approach has come to be the hallmark of modern science, which proved to be so influential on Marx: Science seeks to generate empirical regularities, mathematically expressed as laws and testable through some form of controlled observation. Concepts, in this approach, must be *operationalizeable* to be useful—that is, they must be capable of expression in terms of the physical operations that can be performed upon them. It should be noted that this method is not necessarily inductive: There is no claim that the laws are derived on the basis of observation alone. Rather, as with Galileo, the laws may be derived on the basis of certain assumptions, prior theorizing, mathematical deductions, and even hunches. What is important is that once a law is generated, it is subjected to empirical testing in as objective a fashion as possible.

It was Newton (1642-1727) more than any other figure who provided science with the hope that it might someday explain all phenomena in terms of a relatively small number of mechanical laws. Newton recognized that a single set of equations might suffice to describe such diverse phenomena as planetary motion, colliding balls, falling objects, tidal motion—all that moves, in the heavens as well as on earth. Newton's theory generated equations that expressed the forces between material objects in terms of simple properties of the objects themselves (their mass), the distance between them, and certain constants. By conceiving of forces as acting upon infinitesimal units or packets of mass, Newton was able to sum all such forces into aggregates that represented the motion of large objects as if they were parts of a vast machine. Democritus's dream had finally been realized: In principle, it was now possible to predict future states of matter in light of their present states. In Newton's mechanistic universe, everything is determined and therefore predictable; all that prevents the scientist from becoming an infallible seer is a lack of knowledge concerning the nature of the forces operating at the moment—a shortcoming that will be overcome in due time.

Newtonian mechanics had an enormous impact on all subsequent thinking, particularly that surrounding the emerging sciences of human beings and their institutions. For several hundred years—until the early twentieth century—Newton's mechanistic cosmology dominated scientific thought. The implications were both simple and fundamental. According to Newtonian cosmology, the universe operates according to simple, knowable laws that describe the mechanical interrelationships among independent bodies. As we have previously noted, these interrelationships are conceived as a system of forces that are aggregated from the properties of individual bodies.

Marx was impressed by the promise of Newtonian science. He accepted the basic materialistic premise that the fundamental building blocks of the world consist of things *in* the world, rather than ideas or concepts *about* the world. In a significantly ambivalent way, as we shall see, he was attracted to the idea of predictability. He appreciated the dynamic nature of Newtonian physics, which regarded the universe as a system of bodies in motion complexly interacting upon one another. But he rejected the mechanistic nature of physics: The automatic operation of forces left no room for human purpose or agency. Atoms and planets may act out of a blind, deterministic necessity, but humans, in Marx's view, need not do so. One major concern of Marx's therefore lay in freeing scientific materialism from its mechanistic assumptions. Marx also rejected the methodological individualism of Newtonian physics—the notion that systems are nothing more than the aggregated properties of their constituent parts. He did not fully adopt the position of methodological holism, however, since to believe (as Saint-Simon and Comte did) that the whole determines the properties of the parts would seem to deny the power of the individual to change them. Finally, Marx came to question the Newtonian notion that universal laws can be generated that apply all phenomena. We shall return to these issues in Chapters 5 and 7.

Newtonian physics had an enormous impact on the effort of philosophy to reconcile logos and doxa, idealism and materialism. The French philosopher Descartes, for example, sought to demonstrate that even the seemingly factual knowledge of physics could be derived on the basis of purely mental activity—logical deduction from the self-evident (to Descartes) *cogito*.[7] But not until the Scottish empiricist David Hume (1711-1776) unwittingly demonstrated that experience alone could not produce knowledge was modern idealist philosophy born in the form that was to influence Marx.

Hume, culminating a tradition that includes Hobbes, Locke, and Berkeley, sought to provide a purely empiricist foundation for human knowledge by demonstrating that all of our ideas about the external world could ultimately be grounded in sense experience. Knowledge, according to Hume, consists of concepts, the mental representations of external things. Concepts therefore derive from impressions and ideas, which are in turn caused by real objects. In perception, the flow is from object to sensation to impression to idea;[8] the idea remains long after the object ceases to be present to the senses. Simple impressions can combine to yield complex ideas, but what is important is that we can never directly know the objects that give rise to impressions: "the mind has never anything present to it but the perceptions, and cannot possibly reach any experience of their connection with objects" (1968b: 421). The details of Hume's theory of knowledge need not occupy us, except to note that his insistence that "all reasonings concerning matters of fact seem to be founded on the relation of cause and effect (1968a: 323) led philosophy into a paradoxical dilemma from which Kant, Hegel, and finally Marx sought to extricate it.

Hume reasoned that sensations, by themselves, can provide knowledge only of that which is immediately present to the senses at a specific moment: There must be something else that connects discrete sensations into concepts that have durability across time and space. Hume concluded that such connections are provided by the concept of causation, which alone among concepts "can be traced beyond our senses, and informs us of existences and objects, which we do not see or feel" (1968b: 358). Knowledge of causal relations requires that the causally related events be spatially contiguous, temporally sequential, and—herein lies the paradox—*necessarily* connected. We may observe that A is contiguous to B in space, and that furthermore B is always observed to follow A; but this does not tell us why B *must* follow A, and therefore does not preclude the possibility that at some future time the predicted relationship may in fact not occur. While knowledge of contiguity and succession can be grounded in direct observation, necessity cannot: No amount of observation will reveal the necessary connection between two events. In other words, knowledge based on experience alone can never give rise to concepts about causality; yet without such concepts, knowledge is not possible at all.

Hume in fact offered a psychological solution to this paradox. Having demonstrated that the idea of causation cannot be derived either from pure reason nor from sense-experience, Hume concluded that it must derive from the imagination—or, more precisely, from our psychological need for predictability (i.e., from habit).[9] Such a solution did not offer adequate grounds for philosophical certainty, however, and consequently Hume provided the impulse for subsequent efforts by more idealist philosophers to reassert the importance of purely mental (i.e., nonempirical) concepts as the crucial constitutive elements of factual knowledge.

Kant

The German idealist philosopher Immanuel Kant's (1724-1804) answer to Hume denied the basic empiricist premise that all knowledge must ultimately originate in experience. Although Kant agreed that experience indeed provides the content, he also argued that the structure of the mind itself contributes to knowledge by organizing experience into humanly intelligible categories.

For Kant, the human mind (termed the *organon*) must be constructed in a certain way if knowledge is to be at all possible. For example, if—as Hume demonstrates—so fundamental a concept as *causation* is not directly traceable to experience alone, then it must somehow reside in the mind itself. What features must the mind possess in order to enable us to think and reason as we do? Kant concluded that without certain in-born mental properties, thought would not be possible at all. First, he reasoned, some prior concepts of time and space are necessary: Without the innate ability to intuit the reality of spatio-temporal relations, human thinking could not occur. Therefore, Kant concluded, the mind possesses two innate *forms* of time and space. Second, rational decision making requires a number of basic judgments to be made (Kant used physics and biology to formulate his criteria for such judgments). These judgments, Kant believed, are 12 in number—and they therefore require 12 corresponding innate mental *categories*.[10] For example, Hume was correct in concluding that we can never know about causation from experience alone; what he failed to realize was that our knowledge of causation is not external in origin but rather results from the mind itself. Kant posits the existence of an innate mental capability of knowing causality *prior* to any concrete experience of a cause-and-effect relation, thereby enabling us to organize our experiences under the category of causality. In this formulation, it need not trouble us that one cannot derive causation out of experience alone, since it was there (in the mind) all along. All 12 categories operate in a similar fashion: They reflect concepts that *must* be built into the mind if we are to make judgments at all, since they cannot be obtained from experience.

Prior to Kant, philosophers had generally treated knowledge as deriving from one of two sources: either exclusively from experience, or exclusively from the mind. Empiricists such as Hume believed that knowledge entails a mental combination or synthesis of information obtained after the fact of direct experience; they therefore held knowledge to be *synthetic a posteriori*. Rationalists such as Plato argued that knowledge results from the mental analysis of concepts prior to any experience; they argued, in turn, that knowledge is *analytic a priori*. Kant broke through this dualism by arguing that in fact knowledge entailed a little bit of both: The contents of knowledge derive after the fact of concrete experience, but the forms in which we organize that experience consist of previously existing mental constructs. In other words, knowledge, for Kant, is both synthetic and a priori.

Kant's solution to the problem of knowledge possesses an obvious plausibility. To use somewhat more contemporary terminology, our minds, like computers, are seen by Kant as hardwired in such a fashion as to make possible only certain types of knowledge. Moreover, we have no possibility of any other way of knowing: Our human knowledge necessarily reflects our human mental structures.[11] But Kant's particular formulation contains certain troubling deficiencies, two of which proved significant for the subsequent development of dialectics in philosophy, which in turn paved the way for Marx's effort to construct a dialectical social theory.

First, the relationship between external "facts" and our internal mental ideas about those facts only *seems* to be addressed by Kant. Kant claims that *all* we can ever know about the external world consists of our experiences of that world as *processed* by our innate mental structures. In other words, we can never have direct, unmediated knowledge of the world itself. In Kant's language, the thing-in-itself (or *noumenon,* as he termed it) is by assumption unknowable; all we can know is the thing-for-us (or *phenomenon*), which is the thing-in-itself transformed by our mental apparatus. If this is the case, why posit the existence of a thing-in-itself at all? In Kant's terms, why assume the existence of a noumenal world, if the only world we can ever know is the humanly constituted phenomenal one? This is an important question because unless one can somehow demonstrate a necessary connection between external "fact" and internal idea, then one can never prove that our ideas accurately reflect those facts that are presumably their source. If certain preexisting concepts are indeed an inseparable component of all knowledge, how do I know that the resulting knowledge is not deceptive? As with more thoroughgoing rationalist philosophies, Kant's hybrid rationalism runs the danger of being excessively subjective—a danger that renders it unacceptable to would-be scientists (such as Marx) concerned with developing truly "objective" theories about the external world.[12]

This problem is related to the second one: Kant's solution is both static and arbitrary. Why are there exactly two forms and 12 categories? Why are these fixed for all times, almost like a series of mechanical relays waiting to be triggered? Why does Kant assume that our mental structures cannot evolve to accommodate our changing experiences, in a process whereby mind and experience mutually constitute and condition one another in an ongoing dialectic? A similar difficulty arises from the fact that in Kant's dualistic formulation—which counterposed external noumena to conceptualized phenomena—ethical imperatives are radically separated from scientific facts: A great gulf separates *what is* from *what ought to be.*

Fichte, Hegel, Feuerbach, and Dialectics

Kant's disciple, Johann Gottlieb Fichte (1762-1814), sought to overcome the static and seemingly arbitrary nature of Kant's categories through a theory of action that was to become the cornerstone of Marx's theory of praxis (Garaudy, 1967: 34). Fichte argued that the future must be created through action informed by reason, a process through which human beings fully realize their essential human nature. Garaudy (1967: 35) notes that "it is Fichte's *Doctrine of Science,* with its reflections on the creative action of man, on the primacy of action, on the necessity of the transcendence of the individual in the rational totality, which left its mark on the young Marx."

While Marx had rejected both Kant's and Fichte's purely abstract, philosophical approach to freedom as early as 1837,[13] the latters' influence is nonetheless evident. Freedom, for Fichte, is equated with human activity—with the creation and recreation of a humanized world, in which the fruits of one's actions contribute to the conditions underlying future action. Human existence is not predetermined; nor is it constructed *de novo*, out of whole cloth. Rather, Fichte postulates a dialectical relationship between the antecedents and consequents of action. As Fichte states (in Garaudy, 1967: 38, note 8), "humanity rejects blind chance and the power of fate. It holds its fate in its own hands; it accomplishes freely what it has resolved to do." This freedom includes the ability to recognize that human beings (not God, not nature) are the source of social laws, and that legitimation accordingly rests with the individual. Human beings are therefore given responsibility for making their own history, realizing the synthesis of creation and reason in the continual transcendence of limits. Growth, development, self-making— the goal of human existence is to realize reason practically, that is, not after the abstract fashion of philosophy, but rather through oneself and thence in the external world.

In thus "accomplishing" history, humans collectively transform nature, society, and self. Nature becomes humanized. Furthermore, this process is regarded by Fichte as inherently social: One cannot act in isolation, but rather only in and through others. Rights are not purely individualist, but derive from the community; ethical imperatives originate in society. Fichte extends this analysis, in a limited way, to the institution of private property: While he does not question its universality (as Marx was to do), he does recognize that property has a social dimension resulting from human labor, and that therefore the poor are under no universal ethical imperative to legitimate the property relations that impoverish them.

The German philosopher Georg Wilhelm Friedrich Hegel (1770-1831) sought to bridge the dualities in the philosophies that preceded him, including that between the ethical *ought* and the factual *is*. Hegel agreed with Kant that empiricism erred in attempting to ground all ideas in purely sensory experience. But, like Fichte, he disagreed with Kant's solution—the static, prestructured organon that serves to organize all knowledge into certain universal and unchanging forms. Hegel argued that a true understanding of the world involves comprehending the *relationship* between the subject that perceives and the objects that are perceived. Knowledge emerges through a process of interaction whereby the subject both transforms and is transformed by the object. Subjects are not simply passive receptacles that reflect a presumably objective external world (Hume)—nor do they impose an invariant mapping upon that world (Kant). This is because the relationship between subject and object has a historical or evolutionary component, which must be understood if we are to give an adequate account of the nature of both. What we conventionally term *things* are in fact better understood as *relations:* They can be explained only by situating them within processes of development and change, not only in relation to one another but in relation to changes in the perceiving subject. So-called objects, in other words, can be understood only as parts of larger totalities that include both other objects as well as the subject itself.

Hegel termed his approach for understanding relation, change, and totality *dialectics.*[14] According to Hegel, thought moves by a process of *determinate negation:* Negation because each concept calls forth its opposite, determinate because the opposition is unique to each concept. The most abstract concept, presupposed in all thinking, is that of "being": To think at all one must have the prior notion of pure existence. Yet the notion of being cannot exist by itself; rather, it logically requires a contrary notion to stand alongside, against which it acquires its significance. This notion is its logical opposite, the one concept that implies its complete negation: The concept of nothing or "not-being." To think about being one must simultaneously have the notion of its complete absence, not-being. In Hegel's terminology, *being* is the original thesis, and *not-being* is its antithesis, its determinate negation. These two concepts are logical opposites, contradictorily yet necessarily related; and an understanding of that relationship implies yet a third concept that is *necessarily* implicated in the first two. This concept is that of *becoming:* the passing into or out of being, the movement between being and not-being. When one thinks about being, one must necessarily think about not-being, and this in turn requires one to think about becoming. According to Hegel, the concept becoming is the *synthesis* of the two previous concepts—the fusion of thesis and antithesis in a "higher" concept that encompasses yet goes beyond both. This new synthesis—becoming—itself then becomes a thesis, giving rise to its own negation or antithesis, which leads in turn to a new synthesis between the two. The process then continues ad infinitum, a logical process whereby (Hegel believed) all concepts that exist in our mind inevitably evolve as a direct result of the nature of thought.

Thought, in summary, is seen by Hegel as entailing the unity of opposites: Two contradictory concepts retain their opposition, yet are determinately related and therefore lead ineluctably to yet another concept, which in turn presupposes its own determinate negation, and so on and on. Each thought presupposes all previous thought and calls forth all subsequent thought in an unfolding *process of thought* that moves of its own internal necessity toward total knowledge—Hegel's Absolute Idea (or Spirit, *Geist*) that comprehends all previous ideas, including the knowledge of its own self-development.

Hegel's own historical application of his dialectical method led him to conclude that history is a process whereby an Absolute Idea intervenes in human affairs by shaping all social relations around the idea of freedom. As history unfolds, the current notions of freedom are contradicted by new ones, revolutionary changes result, and the society is reconstituted around a new and "higher" idea of freedom. History is therefore a process whereby societies develop increasingly advanced ideas of freedom, ideas that subsequently pervade and shape relations among all societies. Ultimate human emancipation will come when people understand themselves to be the subjects or authors of this process, and subsequently institutionalize the notion of freedom for all people. Hegel's philosophy is thus a version of philosophical idealism, in that it regards the ultimate source of reality to be the self-movement of the Absolute Idea.

Marx was strongly influenced by Hegel's ideas—particularly the notion that knowledge and history develop in a dialectical process whereby such concepts as freedom, and seemingly discrete institutional realms such as art, law, the economy, family relations, and the state, are all interconnected in an unfolding totality. He accepted Hegel's belief in the evolutionary nature of history, and of the centrality of the human subject in the process of shaping that history. On the other hand, Marx rejected Hegel's belief in the autogenesis of the Idea through a process of determinate negation—the notion that concepts somehow automatically unfold according to fixed and inevitable sequences. Marx rather sought to ground the dialectic in the empirical study of economic institutions, thereby rendering it useful for the study of social processes and institutional change. A vital link was missing between Hegel's dialectic—which moved exclusively at the level of ideas—and the institutional change Hegel purported to explain. Part of this link was provided by Hegel's pupil, Ludwig Feuerbach (1804-1872).

The same year Marx received his doctorate (1841), Feuerbach (1957) published *The Essence of Christianity,* a work that, according to Engels (1841: 18), turned his generation "at once [into] Feuerbachians."[15] Two additional books followed in the next two years, *Provisional Theses for the Reform of Philosophy* and *Principles of the Philosophy of the*

Future, splitting the young Hegelians between supporters of Feuerbach and Bauer. Feuerbach had criticized Hegel for beginning with the abstract rather than the concrete—for making nature secondary to thought. In Feuerbach's view, Hegel had reversed the relationship between nature and consciousness: "The true relation of thought to Being is this: Being is subject, thought is predicate. Thought springs from Being, but Being does not spring from thought" (*Provisional Theses;* quoted in Marcuse, 1969: 269). Nature—not God or Geist—is granted primacy as the source of consciousness. To use Feuerbach's terminology, philosophy must reverse the order of subject and predicate found in Hegel: It must begin with nature, not with the abstract concept. Only thus can true emancipation be found: "The liberation of man requires the liberation of nature" (Marcuse, 1969: 269). Within the rarified world of German idealist philosophy, such thoughts were heretical.

In *The Essence of Christianity* (1957; quoted in Garaudy, 1967: 26), Feuerbach argued that Christianity offers an alienated notion of God:

> Man transforms the subjective, i.e., the actuality of which exists only in his mind, his perception, his imagination, into something existing beyond his thought, his perception, his imagination. . . . Thus the Christians detach the mind and soul of man from his body, and make of this detached spirit, deprived of a body, their God. . . . Man projects a being beyond himself . . . the opposition of the divine and human is an illusory opposition . . . all divine decisions are the decisions of a human being.

Human beings are not alienated from God, as Christianity would have it; rather, the reverse is true. God is nothing more than humanity's idealized version of itself projected onto the heavens and then denied— its alienated essence. Such alienation can be overcome by the transformative method—inverting the order of subject and predicate, thereby restoring the predicates falsely attributed to God back to humanity. Thus, for example, instead of stating that "God is infinite," one should state that "humanity is infinite." Humanity will realize itself only when it frees itself from such religious alienation; it will liberate itself when it recognizes itself as the true subject of the predicates it falsely attributes to God. Furthermore, just as religion inverts the true order of subject and predicate, so too does Hegelian philosophy, which Feuerbach regarded as "true theology" (*Principles,* par. 5; quoted in Garaudy, 1967: 28).

In a comment following the publication of the *Provisional Theses,* Marx offered his general approval of Feuerbach's philosophical system, "except for one point: he directs himself too much to nature and too little to politics. But it is politics that happens to be the only link through which contemporary philosophy can become true" (March 13, 1843, letter to Ruge; quoted in Avineri, 1968: 10). Within two years Marx had come to reject the philosophical system as well. Contrary to Hegel, Feuerbach had regarded the material world as primary, giving rise to our ideas about it: "The object, in its true meaning, is given only by the senses. . . . Nothing is unquestionably and immediately certain except the object of the senses, of perception and sensation" (*Principles,* par. 32, 37; quoted in Marcuse, 1969: 271). Here, however, Feuerbach replaces Hegel's abstract idealism with an equally abstract materialism. Although Marx welcomed Feuerbach's efforts to invert Hegel along materialist premises, he rejected the abstract and deterministic qualities of the Feuerbachian system. Ultimately, Marx eventually concluded, Feuerbach had merely replaced the determinancy of Geist with an equally abstract determinancy of matter. As Marx notes in the 1845 Seventh Thesis on Feuerbach (in McClellan, 1977: 157),

> Feuerbach, consequently, does not see that the "religious sentiment" is itself a social product, and that the abstract individual whom he analyzes belongs to a particular form of society.

What is needed, in other words, is not an abstract inversion of Hegel, but a concrete institutional analysis that applies dialectical reason to the analysis of actual society. By the time of the 1844 *Economic and Philosophical Manuscripts,* Marx had come to argue that alienation results not from religion but from contradictions in the political-economic base of society—and particularly the institution of private property. It followed, then, that alienation could be overcome only by addressing the "secular foundation."[16] In his *Critique of Hegel's Philosophy of Right,* Marx extended Feuerbach's notion of religion-as-alienation to the state as a form of alienation. In Hegel's system, the Prussian state was seen as the political embodiment of Reason, the highest realization of the emergence of the Absolute Idea. Applying Feuerbach's method of "inversion," Marx argued that in fact the reverse was true—that "civil society"[17] produces the state and ideology, rather than the reverse. "The anatomy of civil society is to be sought in political economy" (from the 1859 Preface to *A Critique of Political Economy;* in McClellan, 1977: 389); contrary to Hegel, the state does not somehow stand outside of society, but rather reflects society's property relations.

Scientific Reason and Human Progress

By the eighteenth century it was evident that science was capable of transforming nature; all that remained was to apply Newton's method to social affairs. This was to be accomplished by subjecting society to the same sort of study that physicists had applied so successfully to the study of the natural world. Newton had managed to reduce the complexity of nature to a handful of general laws, thereby bringing it under control; surely the same could be done for society. No longer was a purely deductive metaphysics after the fashion of Descartes or Hume sufficient. True scientific understanding required reason to be grounded in rigorous observation.

The Legacy of the Enlightenment

The Enlightment philosophes adopted a skeptical attitude toward all metaphysical systems. Instead, they empirically studied existing societies in hopes of rationally reconstructing a more perfect one—a society that would permit its members to realize their fullest potential. Montesquieu's (1962) 1748 *Spirit of the Laws,* for example, developed a political typology that correlated different forms of governance with such institutions as education, the legal system, family relationships, and even geography, specifying the sorts of political systems that were appropriate to the various types of society. Condorcet argued that human beings were perfectible, a notion also developed by Rousseau, who believed that existing human institutions stood in the way of perfectibility.

In various ways the French philosophes sought to demonstrate that the social and political order of the *Ancien Regime* needed to be overthrown in order for a truly rational society to be constructed. Their ideas were influential in shaping the climate of opinion in late eighteenth-century France, and ultimately the French Revolution itself. That event, unfortunately, led not to a utopian society, but rather to chaos and anarchy: The wild optimism of the Enlightenment was buried by the guillotine, a reign of terror, and Napoleon. This in turn led to a conservative reaction throughout Europe during the first part of the nineteenth century, with philosophers railing against the Enlightenment notion that societies were merely artificial constructs that could and should be torn asunder and then reengineered.

The philosophes had made the individual citizen the centerpiece of their utopias. Society was seen as an aggregate of individuals, each of whom willingly exchanged some measure of freedom for the benefits of community, which was then judged according to how well it enabled its members to realize their fullest potential. Conservatives such as Bonald, de Maistre, Burke, Saint-Simon, and Comte rejected this individualistic position, arguing instead that the social organism—be it the community, the nation, or the people—was both historically and logically prior to the individual. Edmund Burke, for example, observed that individuals were born into societies the beliefs, customs, and traditions of which predated individuals and would survive them as well: Social institutions belong to this historical legacy, and not to a single generation of would-be revolutionaries. Hegel, as we have seen, similarly saw the evolution of society as an organic development—in this case reflecting the unfolding of the Absolute Idea. The conservative position regards society as an organic unity of interdependent parts, prior to (and ethically superior to) the individual, who is regarded as a subordinate bearer of social roles. Customs and institutions, status and hierarchy are regarded as functional for the survival of the social whole, which is partly assured by necessary ritual, ceremony, and worship (Zeitlin, 1981: 59-60).

Marx drew on both the Enlightenment philosophes and their conservative critics. With the former, for example, he concluded that society can indeed be measured by the extent to which it enables individuals to realize their potential. Marx condemns all existing societies for deforming their members; the task of science is to criticize such deformations, penetrating below society's surface institutions to reveal the structured realities that ultimately cause them. Marx shares the eighteenth-century faith that reason and observation can be combined in scientific inquiry eventually to pave the way for an earthly utopia in which human perfectibility will be realized.

With the conservatives, Marx agreed that societies are like functionally interdependent organisms in which myth, ritual, and religion play important parts. He did not regard societies as unitary organisms, as did the conservatives, however, but rather saw society as divided into economic classes in a state of perpetual warfare. Myth, ritual, and religion were seen as important—not because they reflected some deep wellspring of the human need for order, but because they make up a part of the ideology by which the dominant class keeps the subordinate ones in line.

Furthermore, Marx—like the conservatives—believed that institutions fundamentally shape human behavior through the social roles they provide, although, as we shall see, he also believed that we are capable of shaping our roles and institutions at the same time they shape us. Finally, following Hegel, Marx believed that societies undergo a sort of natural evolution, although he parted company with the conservatives on one crucial point: Evolution becomes revolution once the weaknesses inherent in a given type of society are more-or-less fully manifested.

Political Economy

The seemingly most scientifically advanced social science of Marx's time was economics—the study of the production, distribution, and consumption of goods and services. Adam Smith's (1937) *Wealth of Nations,* published in 1776, perhaps more than any other work seemed to realize the Newtonian promise of a social physics. For one thing, Smith sought to develop a comprehensive general theory that would account for all significant facets of the intersection of politics and economics. Perhaps even more significantly, he sought to provide the new discipline with a quantitative foundation—a system of accounting that would permit the measurement of relationships and the prediction of effects.

As we saw in Chapter 1, early in his life, Marx had concluded that economics is fundamental to the operation of all societies. Whatever the philosophers may think, societies—and their members—must first reproduce themselves at the material level before they can devote much attention to more lofty concerns. The economy thus holds the key to the social system. As early as 1843 Marx was writing on economic issues for the *Rheinische Zeitung,* and the following year—after reading Engels's "Outlines of Political Economy"—he undertook his first systematic study of such classical economists as Smith, Ricardo, Say, Sismondi, James Mill, and others (Kamenka, 1983: lviii).

In Smith's time most economists treated the price of a commodity as reflecting its underlying value, an assumption that permitted them to use price as a universal accounting measure. This, in turn, made it possible to talk about supply and demand throughout the economy in commensurable terms—an important step in giving economics the appearance of an exact quantitative science. Unfortunately, this approach begged a crucial question: Why should the underlying assumption—that price and value are equivalent—be true?

While most economists are no longer troubled by such questions, this was not true of the discipline's founders. Adam Smith in particular was concerned to find the "accurate measure" (1937: 31) of price—that universal measure embodied in commodities that permitted all manner of goods to be compared and exchanged. The clue was provided by Smith's fundamental distinction between *use-value* and *exchange-value.* The former refers to the value of a commodity to its user, while the latter refers to the price that commodity will command in the marketplace. Paradoxically, Smith noted, some of the most useful items (for example, water) have little or no exchange value, while many relatively useless items (for example, diamonds) command a high price. Why should this be the case?

Smith's answer was straightforward: For purposes of measuring value, the common denominator possessed by items in exchange is the amount of labor it takes to produce them. Labor-time, then, is the universal measure that permits diverse products to be equated. "Labour, therefore, is the real measure of the exchangeable value of all commodities. . . . The real price of everything . . . is the toil and trouble of acquiring it" (1937: 30). Labor is the source of the wealth of nations: "The annual labour of every nation is the fund which originally supplies it with the necessities and conveniences of life" (1937: lvii). Market price may fluctuate according to the vagaries of supply and demand, but in the long run labor-time asserts its determining impact on the "natural price . . . to which the prices of all commodities are continually gravitating" (1937: 56-58). This is true not only of the price of labor itself, but of land and capital as well (1937: 50):

> Labour measures the value not only of that part of price which resolves itself into wages, but of that which resolves itself into rent and of that which resolves itself into profits. In every society the price of every commodity finally resolves itself in some one or another, of those three parts.

Smith's labor theory of value, although subsequently abandoned by economists, remained central to Marx's economic theories. Whereas Smith himself focused exclusively on exchange-value, treating it as a virtual proxy for use-value, Marx retained the distinction. Smith, for example, had treated the use-value of labor itself as if it were accurately indexed by its exchange-value (the wage). Marx, on the other hand— taking his clue from Smith—concluded that the use- and exchange-value of labor are very different things: The former consists in the ability of labor to produce new value, while the latter measures only the cost of producing the labor itself. In other words, the worker's wages are sufficient to cover his or her own costs of survival, yet the worker's labor-time is available to the capitalist or landlord for a longer period of time, sufficient for the production of additional commodities the sale of which would enrich not the worker, but the person who controls the worker's labor power. This additional labor-time—devoted to enhancing the profits and rents of others—was termed by Marx *surplus value*. It was one of Marx's seminal discoveries, to which we shall return in Chapter 5.

Marx was critical of classical political economy in another regard: It fails to recognize that its presumably universal laws in fact grow out of—and in turn serve—a particular social order. Political economy, in Marx's view, is not a social physics; rather, it is part science and part ideology. For this reason Marx subjected the claims of political economy to a thoroughgoing critique, which enabled him to assimilate that which was promising to his own economic system, while discarding the remainder as ideological. We will examine Marx's economic theory in some detail in Chapter 5. First, however, we must better understand his use of the critical method that informed his own understanding of political economy. Of special interest is the question of continuity (or discontinuity) in Marx's thinking. Was Marx primarily concerned with developing a critical philosophy throughout his career, as some contend? Or did he abandon such early efforts as mere philosophic speculation, turning instead to the development of a more scientifically based economic theory?

NOTES

1. Habermas (1971: 30) notes that "the *theoros* was the representative sent by Greek cities to public celebrations. Through *theoria,* that is, through looking on, he abandoned himself to the sacred events. In philosophical language, *theoria* was transferred to the contemplation of the cosmos."

2. For discussions of the pre-Socratic Greek philosophers, see Hyland (1973) and the collection of essays in Mourelatos (1974).

3. For example, Pythagoras's well-known theorem relating the sides of a right triangle was taken as evidence of the basically mathematical nature of the cosmos: Why else would an algebraically (hence, mental) derivation exactly describe the physical world? (In fact, of course, Pythagoras's theorem is only approximately true in the curved space-time of the actual universe as it is understood today.)

4. The universal forms, Plato believed, were the source of not only concrete physical objects, but of cultural objects as well—for example, law, art, and ethics. In other words, just as we recognize a living horse as such because we have a preexisting mental concept of "horse," so too we know the truth of certain ethical notions such as equality because they reflect the more universal ethical forms that are resident in the mind.

5. For example, Empedocles argued that earth, air, fire, and water were mixed in various combinations by Love (bringing together) and Strife (driving apart); these combinations give rise to the multiplicity of observed elements.

6. "By convention color exists, by convention bitter, by convention sweet, but in reality atoms and the void" (reported by Galen; in Nahm, 160). *Atom* derives from *a* (un) *tome* (cut), that is, the irreducible particle. While such atomic particles as electrons and protons reflect materialist assumptions, such contemporary theoretical constructs as quarks or two-dimensional strings might seem to be more consistent with the idealist approach of Plato.

7. Descartes's *cogito ergo sum* (I think, therefore I am) sought to develop a factual foundation for philosophy that would satisfy the most committed skeptic. For Descartes, the one fact that cannot be seriously questioned is the fact that I am thinking about doubting; therefore, philosophy begins with the certainty of the thinking self (*cogito*), and deduces all other concepts therefrom.

8. Hume distinguished impressions from ideas: The former are perceptions deriving from immediate (outward or inward) experience, and possess "most force and violence"; the latter are "the faint images of these in thinking and reasoning" (1968b: 298).

9. Hume developed similar arguments concerning the concepts of substance (the notion that an object observed at one time is the same object observed at another time and space) and identity (the preservation of the concept of self across time and space).

10. The 12 judgments, and their corresponding categories, are divided by Kant into four groupings. Concerning *quantity,* the judgments are universal (the corresponding category = unity), particular (= plurality), and singular (= totality); concerning *quality,* affirmative (= reality), negative (= negation), and infinite (= limitation); concerning *relation,* categorical (= substance), hypothetical (= causality), disjunctive (= community); and concerning *modality,* problematic (= possibility-impossibility), assertoric (= existence-nonexistence), and apodictic (= necessity-contingency). For an excellent summary, see Hartnack (1967: Chapter 3).

11. While Kant's specific theory (for example, concerning the two forms and 12 categories) is hardly of scientific interest today, there are many theories that directly or indirectly rely on Kant's basic notion of innate, preexperiential structures that somehow govern human experience. Within psychology, for example, the most prominent neo-Kantian theories are developmental stage theories, such as those of Piaget and Kohlberg.

12. Kant's response might be that so long as all humans share the identical mental apparatus, the question is moot: We may not ever possess a direct knowledge of the thing-in-itself, but we can still develop a universal, shared human knowledge insofar as our identical mental structures are sharpened (presumably through scientific training) to process identical external stimuli in the same clear fashion. This answer, in fact, would lead in the direction of a consensus theory of truth—a lead followed by Habermas (1971: Chapters 5 and 6) in his pragmatically grounded theory of knowledge.

13. "Liberating myself from the idealism I had imbibed from certain elements in the thinking of Fiche and Kant, I arrived at the point of seeking the idea in reality itself" (letter to his father, November 10, 1837; cited in Garaudy, 1967: 34).

14. The dialectical tradition also has classical origins, most notably in the philosophy of Heraclitus.

15. Marx, in fact, was more influenced by Bauer until 1843; his conversion was not so rapid as Engels's quote implies.

16. The fourth Thesis on Feuerbach; see also the 1844 *Manuscripts* and *The German Ideology.* Marx got the idea that private property (and not religion) is the principal source of alienation from Moses Hess (Garaudy, 1967: 30).

17. A term used at the time to denote the private sphere of society, including property relations, the economy in general, and social relations such as the family.

PART II
Marx's Theory

4

Marx and Critique

Much has been written on the topic of whether or not Marx moved from a primary concern with philosophy to one with science during the course of his writing. This debate counterposes two seemingly antithetical interpretations of Marx's work. On the one hand are those who argue that Marx's work is consistently concerned with reification, and that his primary contributions are largely methodological in nature—that is, in developing a critical approach to understanding the relationship between human beings and their ideas as both the objects of historical forces and the sources of those forces. As we noted in Chapter 1, Marx's earliest training was in the Hegelian tradition of philosophical critique—analyzing idea systems to expose their assumptions and inconsistencies, thereby revealing their rational core. The "raw data" of critique is the *concept*. Critique moves at the level of ideas; it shows no interest in systematic data-gathering and hypothesis-testing. "Evidence," when invoked, is anecdotal rather than systematic: The principal concern is with logical consistency, not empirical proof. Critique provides the valuable service of *clarification*—and with it, the *demystification* of previously unquestioned beliefs. One of the earliest versions of this argument was put forth by the Hungarian philosopher Georg Lukacs (1971c), who argued in 1919 that "orthodox Marxism" is nothing more than a method for understanding the genesis and overcoming of reified thought in capitalist society. This interpretation has since been carried forth by the critical theory tradition. Many writers in this tradition, following Lukacs's early lead,[1] argue that not only was the "essential Marx" a philosopher concerned with reification, but that, conversely, his "scientific" writings were lapses in violation of an otherwise strong commitment to critique.

On the other hand, others argue that while Marx began his writing under the influence of philosophy, he soon became primarily concerned with developing a science of the "laws of motion" of capitalist production. The strongest current version of this view is found in the French Marxist structuralist school of Louis Althusser, who has argued that a radical "epistemological break" occurred in Marx's writings in the watershed year of 1845. Before that time, according to Althusser (1969), Marx was concerned with alienation and critique—worthy concerns, to be certain, but not (according to Althusser) amenable to scientific analysis. After "settle[ing] accounts with our erstwhile philosophical conscience" by writing *The German Ideology* in 1845,[2] however, Marx and Engels came to understand that their calling lay in rethinking the science of political economy, rather than in improving on Hegel's philosophical method. Thereafter, according to this reasoning, Marx's work became increasingly concerned with the scientific analysis of underlying social structures, although unfortunate traces of the old humanist concern with reification remain until the very end.

I shall adopt a somewhat intermediate view in arguing that even though Marx's later works are unquestionably primarily concerned with questions of politics and economics, he continued throughout his writings to combat reification through critique. In fact, we shall see in Chapter 5 that Marx's conceptual schema serves a dual function: the generation of empirically verifiable statements, and critique.

The Early Writings

Marx's early work involved transforming and applying Hegel's dialectical method. Whereas Hegel begins with Spirit, Marx begins with people, their activity, and their environment. He then proceeds to examine the classical problems of philosophy and economics.

The 1844 *Economic and Philosophical Manuscripts,* written while Marx was still strongly influenced by Hegel in style as well as substance, serves as a useful example of Marx's use of critique to offer an explanation of the nature and source of alienation in capitalist society. In this unpublished writing,[3] Marx employs Hegelian methodology to situate classical political economy historically—to demonstrate how its static categories are historically limited, unable to penetrate surface appearances, and that therefore "political economy has only expressed the laws of estranged labor" (in McClellan, 1977: 85). Marx shows how classical political economy did not conceive of labor and property as features of capitalism that are intrinsically connected to one another; it therefore cannot account for the historical origins of either, and so falls back on regarding them as universal features of all societies. "Political Economy starts with the fact of private property, it does not explain it to us" (in McClellan, 1977: 77).

Political economy assumed that private property was natural and therefore universal. It expresses in abstract formulas the processes through which private property in capitalist society is produced, distributed, and consumed, formulas which it then takes for universally valid laws. Political economy did not account for the origin of these laws, that is, it did not demonstrate how they arise from the very nature of private property itself, a deficiency Marx seeks to rectify—in Hegelian fashion—by analyzing the concept of labor under capitalism:

> We began with a fact of political economy, the alienation of the worker and his production. We have expressed this fact in *conceptual* terms: *alienated, externalized* labor. We have *analyzed this concept,* and thus analyzed a purely economic fact. [in McClellan, 1977: 83; emphasis added]

Marx begins this analysis by positing labor as the defining attribute of the human species. As a feature of our human essence, or "species-being,"[4] labor is equated with "vital activity . . . productive life itself" (in McClellan, 1977: 82). Labor is conceived by Marx as the key mediation between people and nature whereby people transform nature and are themselves transformed in the process.

In dialectically conceiving of labor as a process of mutual transformation (people/nature)—rather than as an unchanging category—Marx is then able to derive analytically the concept of *alienated* labor, a circumstance in which human labor becomes externalized or *objectified* and stands against us, hostile and controlling. The products of our labor, in other words, can be taken away from us and used as instruments of our own domination. This alienation is what accounts for the historical emergence of private property. Methodologically, what Marx has done is to analyze logically the nature of the labor process, leading him to conclude that as consequence of this process, private property was able to emerge as a particular historical form. In a similar fashion, he then proceeds to derive logically other features of capitalist economics that, like private property, the political economists take as natural:

> Just as we have discovered the concept of private property through an analysis of the concept of alienated, externalized labor, so all categories of political economy can be deduced with the help of these two factors. We

shall recognize in each category of market, competition, capital, money only a particular and developed expression of these first two fundamental elements. [in McClellan, 1977: 86]

In similar fashion, Marx deduces the many interrelated facets of alienation from an analysis of the concept of labor: alienation from the products of one's labor, from the labor process, from one's fellow, and, ultimately, from human nature itself. Alienation from one's product results from the fact that what workers produce can be taken by others and used as an instrument of the workers' own domination. This domination takes several forms. Most obviously, workers produce the very machinery that, in Marx's view, is then used to enslave them and their children. Labor produces capital, the principal means of domination in capitalist society. Less obviously, workers' products in capitalist society take the form of commodities that are bought and sold for a profit: Workers may produce the society's wealth, yet in order to enjoy the fruits of that wealth they must first buy back the very commodities that their labor has produced. Workers in Marx's time were held to starvation wages while they produced a degree of wealth never before seen in history. Finally, the very existence of a commodity society creates additional demands for consumption: Even when our subsistence requirements are satisfied, we become prisoners of a vicious cycle of work and consumerism, slaves to the products we produce.[5]

The second source of alienation, from the labor process, stems from Marx's belief (at least in the *Manuscripts*) that humans realize their potential in conscious, goal-oriented activity—a dialectic of thought and action. This is what distinguishes human beings from lesser animals:

The animal is immediately one with his vital activity. It is not distinct from it. They are identical. Man makes his vital activity itself into an object of his will and consciousness. . . . It is true that the animal, too, produces. It builds itself a nest, a dwelling, like the bee, the beaver, the ant, etc. But it only produces what it immediately needs for itself or its offspring; it produces one-sidedly whereas man produces universally; it produces only under the pressure of immediate physical need whereas man produces freely from physical need and only truly produces when he is thus free. [in McClellan, 1977: 82]

Marx was to reassert his belief in human nature as characterized by a capacity for self-conscious activity almost a quarter-century later, in Volume I of *Capital* (1967: part III, Chapter VII, section 1, p. 178):

A spider conducts operations that resemble those of a weaver, and a bee puts to shame many an architect in the construction of her cells. But what distinguishes the worst of architects from the best of bees is this, that the architect erects his structure in imagination before he erects it in reality. At the very end of every labour-process, we get a result that already existed in the imagination of the labourer at its commencement.

Alienation occurs because, under capitalism, this free, vital activity is lost: Workers produce under compulsion, and with no control over the labor process at all. Instead of this being an end in itself, alienated labor "makes [man's] vital activity and essence a mere means to his existence" (in McClellan, 1977: 82). The labor process is fractionalized and rationalized, with workers reduced to the status of appendages to machines—to mere human forms of physical capital.[6] Conscious control over the labor process rests with the managers.[7]

This suggests a third form of alienation: from one's fellow workers. Marx believed human beings to be fundamentally sociable creatures who derive enjoyment from cooperative enterprises oriented toward common, consciously derived goals. Capitalism, Marx argued, denies this essential sociability, pitting worker against worker in the competition for scarce jobs, and worker against capitalist in a continual fight for control over both the labor process and the fruits of the workers' production.

Finally, all three forms of alienation are different aspects of alienation from human nature itself—what Marx, following Feuerbach, termed *species-being*. Human beings have tremendous potential to achieve joy in their labor, so long as that labor is cooperative, conscious, and free; aimed at the common good; and under the workers' own control. This potential is negated in all class societies. Under capitalism in particular we become stultified and dull, losing our essential humanity as we are increasingly reduced to the status of machines. To reverse this state of affairs—to restore full human potential—one must abolish the division of labor, and thereby alienation. This cannot be done without first abolishing private property and class society—a conclusion Marx had already drawn in his 1843-1844 *Critique of Hegel's Philosophy of Right,* when he announced his discovery of the proletariat as the universal "class with radical chains . . . formed [not] by the poverty produced by natural laws but by artificially induced poverty . . . [demanding] the negation of private property" (in McClellan, 1977: 72-73).

This brief review of Marx's early theory of alienation is instructive on two accounts. First, it suggests the ways in which Marx grounded Hegel's dialectic in the labor process rather than in the self-movement of ideas.[8] In other words, Marx retained from Hegel such primal notions as *process* and *relation,* while rejecting the peculiarly Hegelian belief that social change results exclusively from negation in thought. Rather, in Marx's Feuerbachian inversion of Hegel, social change is to be sought in the processes and relations embedded in social conditions themselves.

Second, these early writings reveal a theory of human nature with tremendous implications for political practice. If indeed human beings possess a certain universal potential as part of their species-being, then is it not reasonable to conclude that social systems which deny that potential will somehow produce widespread disenchantment among their members? Would not workers be ripe for revolution even in times of relative abundance, since their alienation would entail much more than economic privation? An adequate standard of living would be no guarantor of political stability, since presumably workers would still chafe at alienating jobs which denied their potential for free, joyful, cooperative labor. The subjective component of alienation would remain even when objective conditions improved.

There is no evidence that Marx himself drew these conclusions. On the contrary, in his subsequent works this subjective theory of alienation is displaced by a far greater attention to the objective conditions which Marx believed contribute to economic instability and material privation. It is the latter—rather than discontent resulting from unrealized human potential—that Marx chooses to focus on, at least in his completed works (such as *Capital*). Within two years Marx was no longer writing in Feuerbachian terms of a universal human nature, but rather in the more sociological language of the sixth *Thesis on Feuerbach:*

> Feuerbach resolves the religious essence into the human essence. But the human essence is no abstraction inherent in each single individual. In reality it is the ensemble of the social relations. [in McClellan, 1977: 157]

This belief that human nature is sociologically malleable is consistent with Marx's concern for developing a theory of capitalist economics, in which the sources of change are to be found in structural instability and political action rather than in human nature. A focus on human nature might have led Marx to the microanalysis of change, focusing, for example, on such issues as psychological resistance to overcoming alienation. It is obvious that Marx did not move in this direction. Instead, I believe, he recognized the limitations of the purely abstract analysis reflected in the *Manuscripts* and other early writings, but at the same time he did not choose to move in the direction of psychology.[9] Marx's preferred level of analysis was macro rather than micro, and so his units of analysis were social institutions, classes, and whole societies, rather than individuals. Moreover, given the limitations of a pure critique, Marx was inevitably led to the concrete study of actual political economies—to reading and rereading the major economic theorists of his time, and to the 10-year study of British economic statistics that preceded *Capital*. Nonetheless, as we shall see immediately below, Marx's shift in emphasis away from a theory of human nature did not lead him to abandon such concerns altogether: Fifteen years later (in the *Grundrisse*), he would write again of the inherent pleasure in creative, social labor.

Continuities in Critique

Although Marx's post-1846 work generally reveals a central concern with empirically grounded macroeconomic theory, he did not entirely forego critique. Rather, Marx continues to employ critique for the purpose of clarification—both of his own thinking (as in the *Grundrisse*), and in order to penetrate the "mist-enveloped regions"[10] of reified thought in his audience (as in Volume I of *Capital*). Let us take up these two instances in turn.

The Grundrisse

The *Grundrisse*[11]—the 900 pages of notes compiled by Marx during the period 1857-1858—provides valuable insight into his thought as he developed the ideas that were to appear in Volume I of *Capital* nearly a decade later. The *Grundrisse* encompasses the full breadth of his projected economic theory[12] in unpolished form; it reveals a movement between economic and philosophical categories that is largely missing from *Capital*.[13] In the following discussion we will first consider Marx's critique of alienation, next his discussion of the impact of automation on capitalist economies, and finally his reflections on methodology. All three of these instances provide useful insights into Marx's ongoing use of critique in his own self-clarification.

In his discussion of *alienation,* Marx returns to one of his earliest themes, now refracted through the prism of 15 years of economic research. It is therefore especially interesting to note that in key respects his earlier views have changed but little. Much of Marx's discussion recasts his earlier argument from the *Manuscripts* in terms of the labor theory of value (see Chapter 3). While Marx continues to talk of labor objectifying itself in alienated form, he is principally concerned to show that labor is the source of all value, including capital, and that as a consequence labor produces the conditions for its own domination. Marx first notes that labor produces a *surplus value* (beyond the value of goods necessary for its own subsistence):

The point is that the working time necessary for the satisfaction of absolute necessities leaves some free time (which varies at the various stages of the development of the productive forces), so that surplus produce can thus be created if surplus labor is done. [in McClellan, 1977: 369]

This surplus value is then alienated from the worker and used as a means of his or her enslavement:

Now this surplus labor appears objectified as surplus product, and this surplus product, in order to valorize itself as capital, divides itself into a double form: as objective labor conditions (material and instrument) and as subjective labor conditions (food) for the living labor now to be put to work.... All the factors which were opposed to the living labor power as forces which were alien, external, and which consumed and utilized the living labor power under definite conditions which were themselves independent of it, are now established as its own product and result. [pp. 365-366]

In other words, labor experiences a twofold enslavement at its own hands: First, it is enslaved to the capital produced by an earlier generation of workers; and second, it is enslaved by the need to buy back its subsistence goods—commodities also produced by labor. In Marx's earlier (1844) formulation, these two forms of enslavement refer to labor's alienation from both the labor process and its products.

In this same discussion, Marx reveals that he has not completely abandoned his earlier theory of human nature. Marx explicitly rejects Adam Smith's "philosophical view of labor" as "Jehova's curse" (in McClellan, 1977: 368), arguing that

the individual, in his "normal state of health, strength, activity, skill, and efficiency,"[14] might also require a normal portion of work, and of cessation from rest. [p. 368]

Marx here conceives of work as defined in physics—the use of energy to overcome resistance—and further argues that

the overcoming of such obstacles may itself constitute an exercise in liberty, and that these external purposes [obstacles] lose their character of mere natural necessities and are established as purposes which the individual himself fixes. The result is the self-realization and objec-tification of the subject, therefore real freedom, whose activity is precisely labor. [p. 368]

Human beings therefore rejoice in work, so long as

(1) it is of a social nature, (2) it has a scientific character and at the same time is general work, i.e., if it ceases to be human effort as a definite, trained natural force, gives up its purely natural, primitive aspects and becomes the activity of a subject controlling all the forces of nature in the production process. [p. 368]

Under such conditions—labor as socially organized activity over which the worker exerts conscious control—"work is a positive, creative activity" (p. 370). Marx offers two examples: the "composing of music" and the "semi-artistic worker of the Middle Ages" (p. 368).

In sum, Marx appears to be reiterating his earlier notion of people as possessing a universal human nature that is progressively stunted under capitalism, and that therefore might be expected to resist such dehumanization.

Marx expands on this theme in his analysis of automation, which he sees as carrying this process of dehumanization to its fullest extent. Just as labor becomes ever more deskilled, unsocial, and subject to capital's dominion, so does capital also develop a life of its own. In Marx's view, automation—the final stage of capitalism—consists of "a motive force that moves of its own accord" (p. 373). Unlike the tool, which was animated by the "skill and activity" of the worker, the automated machine

> possesses skill and force in the workers' place, is itself the virtuoso. . . . The workers' activity, limited to a mere abstraction, is determined and regulated on all sides by the movement of the machinery, not the other way round. [p. 373-374]

Science itself becomes incorporated into production as a force hostile to labor:

> Science thus appears, in the machine, as something alien and exterior to the worker. . . . The tendency of capital is thus to give a scientific character to production, reducing direct labor to a simple element in this process. [p. 375]

This has enormous implications for the labor theory of value, since it implies that labor ceases to be the source of value in production:

> The production process has ceased to be a labor process in the sense that labor is no longer the unity dominating and transcending it . . . . The value objectified in machinery appears as a prerequisite, opposed to which the valorizing power of the individual worker disappears, since it has become infinitely small.

Direct labor and its quantity cease to be the determining element in production and thus in the creation of use value. It is reduced quantitatively to a smaller proportion, just as qualitatively it is reduced to an indispenseable but subordinate role as compared with scientific labor in general, the technological application of the natural sciences, and the general productive forces arising from the social organization of production. [pp. 375-376]

Marx predicts that "invention then becomes a branch of business," transforming

the workers' operations more and more into mechanical operations, so that, at a certain point, the mechanism can step into his place. . . . Labor does not seem any more to be an essential part of the process of production. The human factor is restricted to watching and supervising the production process. [pp. 379-380]

Labor ceases to be the principal source of wealth; labor-time is no longer the unit of calculus for exchange; and surplus labor need no longer be extracted to develop wealth in general. Science and technology, harnessed to industry, have freed humans from the compulsion to work; "The counterpart of this reduction is that all members of society can develop their education in the arts, sciences, etc., thanks to the free time and means available to all" (p. 380). Unfortunately, this utopian possibility cannot be realized under capitalism—which continues to require universal labor at the same time it renders labor unnecessary. The result is tremendous "alienation, estrangement, and abandonment" (pp. 384-385).

Marx appears to be saying that under such conditions the illogical nature of such a system is self-evident, and that workers—recognizing that their alienated labor is no longer required as a precondition for producing wealth—will overturn the system that has become superfluous. This view is consistent with the earlier one of the *Manuscripts,* which emphasized the subjective experience of alienation rather than the structured instability of the economy. Alienation and perception return to Marx's analysis: Capitalist economic relations are threatened because workers come to understand that they have been rendered unnecessary, rather than because subsocial economic processes have produced some inevitable collapse.[15]

Finally, in a section that offers some rare reflections on methodology, Marx argues against the empiricism of classical economic theory, which believed its concepts to be inductively grounded observed facts. Marx argued that even so basic a notion as "population" cannot be understood outside a more general theoretical framework (in McClellan, 1977: 351):

It seems to be the correct procedure to commence with the real and the concrete, the actual prerequisites; in the case of political economy, to commence with population, which is the basis and the author of the entire productive activity of society. Yet on closer consideration it proves to be wrong.

Population turns out, on reflection, to be an empty abstraction: Population cannot be understood without knowing something about the classes which it comprises, which in turn requires some notions of wage-labor, capital, exchange, money, value, price, and in fact the various elements of economic theory (p. 351):

> If we start out, therefore, with population, we do so with a chaotic conception of the whole, and by deeper analysis we will gradually arrive at simpler ideas; thus we shall proceed from the imaginary concrete to less and less complex abstractions, until we arrive at the simplest determinations. This once attained, we might start on our return journey until we finally came back to population, but this time not as a chaotic notion of an integral whole, but as a rich aggregate of many determinations and relations.

Concepts thus result from a theoretical labor, rather than from simple induction. What appears to be concrete or real in fact becomes so only because we have applied our conceptual scheme to it:

> The concrete is concrete because it is a combination of many determinations, i.e., a unity of diverse elements. In our thought it therefore appears as a process of synthesis, as a result, and not as a starting-point, although it is the real starting point and, therefore, also the starting point of observation and conception. [p. 352]

Thus it is, Marx concludes, that "abstract definitions lead to the reproduction of the concrete subject in the course of reasoning"(p. 352). Marx goes on to argue that even the possibility of this sort of abstract reasoning is first made possible only in a social system "where there is the highest concrete development, where one feature appears to be jointly possessed by many and to be common to all. Then it cannot be thought of any longer in one particular form" (p. 354). The apogee of such a social system is, of course, contemporary bourgeois society, in which labor becomes completely abstracted from any particular context, since capitalism, according to Marx's analysis, deskills all workers and hence renders them interchangeable. This abstract quality of labor as universal labor power is visible for the first time under capitalism precisely because it becomes so highly developed; and this visibility in turn permits one to develop an understanding of less technologically developed social systems in which the abstract quality of labor may not be so self-evident.

> The anatomy of the human being is the key to the anatomy of the ape. But the intimations of a higher animal in lower ones can be understood only if the animal of the higher order is already known. The bourgeois economy furnishes a key to the ancient economy, etc. [p. 355]

Thus, to summarize, Marx is making a twofold statement about the status of his scientific concepts: first, that they derive from theory rather than from direct observation; and second, that theorizing is for the first time made possible by a social system based on highly abstracted social relations. The first statement anticipates the refutation of logical positivism one hundred years later;[16] the second, Mannheim's views on the social origins of knowledge. Both statements result from Marx's use of critique to question conventional epistemologies.[17]

Capital

Although Volume I of *Capital* is primarily concerned with an analysis of capitalist economic production, Marx continues to rely on critique for conceptual clarification—for example, in revealing the relationship between the seemingly natural commodity and the economic system that produces it. Marx comments on his approach in his preface to the first German edition of *Capital,* in which he notes that unlike the scientist, who can rely on instruments to reveal the inner workings of molecules, the economist must proceed by the "force of abstraction":

> In the analysis of economic forms, moreover, neither microscopes nor chemical reagents are of use. The force of abstraction must replace both. But in bourgeois society the commodity-form of the product of labor—or the value-form of the commodity—is the economic cell form. [in McClellan, 1977: 416]

Philosophic critique continues to play a central role in *Capital,* which moves simultaneously on two levels. On one level, it offers an empirically grounded analysis of the structures that underlie capitalist economic relations, in an effort to derive laws that reveal probable developmental tendencies. This reflects Marx's concern for developing a scientific understanding of the "economic law of motion" of capitalism (from Preface to the first edition of *Capital;* in McClellan, 1977: 417). On the second level, *Capital* entails a critique of consciousness: primarily of the supposedly scientific categories of classical political economy, but of popular ideology as well. *Capital* is therefore appropriately subtitled "A Critique of Political Economy." It thus serves an important didactic purpose: It breaks through the reifications whereby people bestow natural qualities on a world they themselves actually produce.

Critique thus entails a dissolution of the seeming reality of our conceptual categories: To criticize is to render transparent the origins of "facts." To achieve such transparency, a seeming fact must be situated within a concrete sociohistorical totality: Only thus can its real nature be understood. Hegel's critical method began with an immediate concept (Being), and then commenced to reconstruct the totality of human consciousness. Marx's method in Volume I of *Capital* is to begin with a seemingly factual object (the commodity) and then to reconstruct the nexus of social relationships that account for its apparent facticity. The purpose of Hegel's method was to achieve freedom from constraints on consciousness; Marx's intention was to destroy the appearance of "naturalness" of the existing social order, making it possible for people to gain control over the conditions that help to shape their lives.

The very structure of Volume I of *Capital* reveals Marx's critical intent. Marx opens the volume (in McClellan, 1977: 421) with the following words:

> The wealth of those societies in which the capitalist mode of production prevails presents itself as an "immense accumulation of commodities," its unit being a single commodity. Our investigation must therefore begin with the analysis of a commodity.

The commodity is the fundamental unit of capitalism—at once its atomic particle and most obvious (and unquestioned) form. If Marx can successfully demystify capitalism at this, its most obvious point, he may also hope to unravel some of its deeper mysteries. Part I of Volume I is therefore concerned with commodities and money, the two most self-evident forms of *Capital*. The transformation of commodities and money into capital is explained in part II, after which Marx devotes the bulk of the remainder of the volume (parts III through VI) to an analysis of the exploitation of labor. These chapters offer a critique of conventional economic theory in order to develop the notion of surplus value (see Chapter 5), which is achieved partially through a detailed historical account of the conflict between labor and capital over the extent and intensity of labor exploitation. This critique also serves to develop the conceptual scheme that serves in Marx's scientific analysis of the "economic law of motion" of capitalist accumulation, which is contained in the final two parts of Volume I (VII and VIII).

Marx's most often-cited use of critique in Volume I is contained in the discussion of "commodity fetishism." A principal concern of this opening chapter is to convince the reader that the sales price of a commodity does not reflect its value (as is commonly presupposed), but rather results from a complex system of social relations that can be understood only through a detailed analysis of capitalist production.[18] In other words, behind the appearance of a quantitative relationship among products lies a "specific, historically conditioned [social] relation between producers" (Sweezy, 1942: 25). In order to make this argument, Marx must first begin by shattering the reader's commonsense notion about the commodity—that it is a tangible, concrete object the value of which is given by its price. Marx therefore begins *Capital* with a chapter on the commodity form, first criticizing its taken-for-granted nature and then reconstructing the concept in light of the complex of capitalist economic relations which he believes alone render it meaningful. Marx begins by seeking to demonstrate how something as seemingly real and tangible as a commodity—the basic unit under capitalism—is quite different from what it initially appears to be (*Capital,* Vol. I; in McClellan, 1977: 435-436):

> A commodity appears, at first sight, a very trivial thing, and easily understood. Its analysis shows that it is, in reality, a very queer thing, abounding in metaphysical subtleties and theological niceties.
>
> A commodity is therefore a mysterious thing, simply because in it the social character of men's labour appears to them as an objective character stamped upon the product of that labour; because the relation of the producers to the sum total of their own labour is presented to them as a social relation, existing not between themselves, but between the products of their labour.
>
> There it is a definite social relation between men, that assumes, in their eyes, the fantastic form of a relation between things.
>
> This Fetishism of commodities has its origin, as the foregoing analysis has already shown, in the peculiar social character of the labour that produces them.

What Marx means by this last sentence is that the apparent social relationship between two inanimate objects (the fact that two commodities exchange for one another) is due to the fact that both were produced by human labor under a specific social organization of production. It is the amount of labor-time embodied in a product that, in the long run and under competitive conditions, determines the rate at which it will exchange for another.[19] Marx then proceeds to show how something as seemingly simple as commodity exchange presupposes a complex system of economic and political relations—how the laws governing exchange are contained not in the objects of exchange but rather in an interdependent system of production, distribution, and consumption.

Problems in the Theory of Consciousness

I have argued that contrary to Marx's assertion that he and Engels had settled their accounts with their "erstwhile philosophical conscience"[20] by 1845, in fact he continued to draw heavily on his legacy of philosophic critique—both methodologically in his scientific analysis, and as his principal means of attacking reified thought. Although we will see in the next chapter that in his later writings Marx increasingly emphasized what he regarded as scientific inquiry in place of critique, he nonetheless continued to give great weight to the importance of conscious action—and therefore continued to rely on critique as essential to breaking down the reifications of both political economy and everyday life.

Marx, influenced both by Enlightenment and Hegelian rationalism, expresses a certain ambivalence concerning the role of reason in history. On the one hand, as we shall see in the next chapter, he often wrote as if macrolevel structural changes would carry history along of their own accord, quite independently of the will and even perceptions of human actors. On the other hand, as I have emphasized in this chapter, Marx also devotes considerable attention to demystifying conventional thought through the use of critique, writing as if critical understanding were a necessary precondition for effective revolutionary action. Moreover, such understanding is to be obtained by the "method of abstraction" whereby logical analysis of a seemingly simple set of ideas reveals their dependence on a system of background assumptions and interrelated concepts. In one sense, Marx is simply extending the legacy of idealist philosophy since Plato, who first equated freedom with truth. As a materialist, however, Marx also looked backward to the socioeconomic origins of false ideas, as well as forward to the realization of correct ideas in practice. Pure criticism is never sufficient.

At the same time, Marx's views on the importance of reason today might appear naively simplistic. Marx believed that critique would break the barriers of reified thought; correct action would inevitably follow. Since people are by nature reasonable, he apparently assumed, they would change their thinking if presented with convincingly logical reasons to do so. First, show the proletariat that its current way of thinking runs counter to its self-interest; then follow up with an alternative set of ideas that both passes scientific muster and better serves their interests. In the best utilitarian tradition, Marx held that people will choose to act in their enlightened self-interest, if only given the necessary information to make the decision, and the opportunity to follow through. It is clear that Marx was wrong in making such strong assumptions. Even critical philosophers do not necessarily make rational choices when it comes to their personal lives. Our most deep-seated beliefs often prove remarkably resilient to reasoned analysis; as Freud recognized, there is a fine line between rationality and rationalization, one that most of us can better discern in others than ourselves. Marx should not be faulted for his naivete: It took the First World War, the rise of fascism in Germany, and the advent of Freudian psychology to render acceptable the belief that human beings more often respond to stirrings far more primal than the supposedly rational processes of the cognitive mind.

The apogee of Marxist critical philosophy was reached in the writings of the Hungarian philosopher Georg Lukacs (1971b), who in 1919 sought to demonstrate that the proletariat was the one class whose concerted actions could alter the course of history, and whose strategic social location guaranteed its eventual success in breaking through the reifications that at the time obscured its sense of history. The details of Lukacs's analysis need not concern us here. We should note, however, that his methodology consisted of a dense philosophical critique that in his view proved conclusively that the proletariat alone could break through the subject-object split that (in Lukacs's view) had proven an insuperable barrier to dereification in the past. However compelling his proof on logical grounds, Lukacs's predictions soon proved wrong; critique alone—even at the hands of a master critic—was not enough. The future of Marxist critical theory was to be found in the theory of consciousness never attempted by Marx. The task of creating such a theory fell to the Frankfurt School, which combined Marxism, cultural analysis, and Freudian theory in an effort to account for reified thinking in interwar Germany in particular, and in popular culture more generally. While an examination of the Frankfurt School is beyond the scope of this book,[21] I believe that their efforts were not entirely successful either. Marxism has yet to develop a theory of consciousness worthy of its economic and political theory.

NOTES

1. Lukacs has since recanted his early position; see his 1967 preface to the new edition of his works (1971a).

2. The quote is from the autobiographical retrospective in Marx's preface to the 1859 *A Critique of Political Economy;* in McClellan (1977: 390).

3. The *Manuscripts* are actually Marx's notebooks from his early reading of several of the classical works in political economy. See Chapter 1.

4. *Gattungswesen,* a term used by Feuerbach.

5. While Marx does not analyze this extensively in the *Economic and Philosophical Manuscripts,* he touches on the concept in *The German Ideology,* and then in greater detail 15 years later in the *Grundrisse.* It is interesting to note that Marx anticipated consumerism at a time when most workers barely earned enough to survive.

6. Marx was later to call labor "variable capital"; see Chapter 5.

7. Although Marx was writing at a time when some degree of control over the labor process still remained in the hands of skilled workers, he anticipated the eventual reduction of labor to its simplest, unskilled form, in which it could be completely controlled as just another capital input into production (see below, discussion of the *Grundrisse*). This vision was finally made explicit as a management ideal with the advent of Frederick Winslow Taylor's theories of scientific management at the turn of the century. See, e.g., Braverman (1974).

8. Actually, Hegel in his early philosophy (the so-called Jenenser system of 1802-1806 offered a highly parallel formulation); see Marcuse, *Reason and Revolution* (New York, 1969: 73-80).

9. Psychology as a science of course did not exist in Marx's time. For example, Freud—whose approach has proven most congenial to Marxists—did not begin to develop his ideas until nearly a half century after Marx developed his own.

10. From *Capital: Volume I,* in McClellan (1977: 436).

11. While all references are to the excerpts in McClellan (1977), Nicolaus's excellent (and complete) translation is also available (Marx, 1973). It should be recalled that the *Grundrisse* was not published until 1941 and was not generally available until the publication of the German edition in 1953. The title *Grundrisse der Kritik der Politischen Okonomie* (Foundation for a Critique of Political Economy) was chosen in 1939 by the editors of the Soviet Marx-Engels-Lenin Institute, reflecting various references in Marx's correspondence (Nicolaus, 1973: 24).

12. Marx divided his "Economics" into six parts, all of which are reflected in the *Grundrisse:* capital, landed property, wage-labor, the state, international trade, and the world market (see Nicolaus, 1973: 54). Of these projected six parts, Marx actually addressed only the first, which grew into four volumes: the three volumes of *Capital* (of which only the first was completed by Marx himself), and *Theories of Surplus Value.* See Chapter 1.

13. Althusser argues that the reduced significance of critique in *Capital* versus the earlier *Grundrisse* reflects Marx's maturation as a scientist—rather than merely the lessened concern with demystification (vis-à-vis economic theory) in the latter, as I argue.

14. This phrase is from Smith.

15. In fact, Marx's analysis in the Grundrisse is somewhat confusing on this point, since immediately after the analysis summarized above, he goes on to argue that the relevance of the declining role of labor lies in the impact that such a decline will have on the long-term profitability of capitalist production, rather than its effect on ideology. See McClellan (1977: 386-387), also Chapter 5, below.

16. See Suppe (1974: 125-191).

17. For further discussion of this point, see Habermas (1975), "The Place of Philosophy in Marxism."

18. In Marx's terminology, why the exchange value is taken to be a measure of the use value (see Chapter 3). A product becomes a *commodity* when it enters into exchange—that is, when it has a price.

19. This is a fundamental premise of classical political economy—the labor theory of value. Marx accepted and extended this premise. We will discuss this in greater detail in Chapter 5.

20. See note 2 above.

21. For a detailed account of the origins and development of critical theory in the Frankfurt School, see Jay (1973); for an excellent summary of its research, see Held (1980).

5

Marx and Science

Marx's desire to develop a unified science of humanity and nature was expressed as early as 1844, when he wrote that "natural science will later comprise the science of man just as much as the science of man will embrace natural science: there will be one single science" (1844 *Manuscripts;* in McClellan, 1977: 94). Marx's view of the fundamental unity of the natural and social sciences—what Habermas (1971: 4) refers to as "orthodox scientism"—entails one of the fundamental assumptions of positivism (see Chapter 2); I shall argue, however, that Marx's methodological self-understanding is not consistent with his actual theoretical approach. In the present chapter we examine Marx's efforts to develop his own scientific understanding of modern society.

MARX AND THE "NATURAL SCIENCE MODEL": SOME AMBIGUITIES

Marx's Empiricist Self-Understanding

While Marx undertook no systematic study of the natural sciences (that task, for better or worse, fell to Engels), it is clear that he had an essentially empiricist view of their procedures (see Chapters 2 and 3), and that, furthermore, he felt that the natural sciences were an appropriate model for his own emerging science of history. In the 1844 *Economic and Philosophical Manuscripts,* Marx comments that "sense experience (see Feuerbach) must be the basis of all science" (in McClellan, 1977: 94). Almost 25 years later, in the preface to the first

German edition of *Capital,* Marx comments that "it is the ultimate aim of this work to lay bare the economic law of motion of modern society" (in McClellan, 1977: 417). In the afterword to the second German edition (published in 1872), Marx approvingly quoted a Russian reviewer, who, discussing Marx's method, observed that

> consequently, Marx only troubles himself about one thing: *to show, by rigid scientific investigation, the necessity of determinate orders of social conditions, and to establish, as impartially as possible, the facts that serve him for fundamental starting-points.* For this it is quite enough if he proves, at the same time, both the *necessity* of the present order of things, and the necessity of another order into which the first must inevitably pass over; and this is all the same, whether men believe it or do not believe it, *whether they are conscious or unconscious of it.* Marx treats the social movement as a process of natural history, *governed by laws not only independent of human will, consciousness, and intelligence, but rather, on the contrary, determining that will, consciousness, and intelligence....* In his opinion, every historical period has laws of its own.... As soon as society has outlived a given period of development, and is passing over from one given stage to another, it begins to be subject also to other laws. [in McClellan, 1977: 419; emphasis added]

"What else," Marx asked, "is he [the reviewer] picturing but the dialectical method?" (in McClellan, 1977: 420).

This quotation, replete with references to blind laws, inevitable results, and objective facts, would please the most hard-nosed empiricist. In fact, Marx's only retreat from arguing that societies are governed by universal laws would appear to be the concluding caveat that laws are situationally specific: Different laws are seen as applying to different historical periods, as when Marx, in his critique of Malthus, observed that "every special historic mode of production has its own special laws of population, historically valid within its limits alone" (*Capital: Volume I,* 1967: 632). This modification enables those such as Szymanski (1973), who fancy Marx as a natural scientist, to accord him a greater affinity for biology than physics or chemistry: Marx believed the laws of the latter to be universal while the former were species-specific. Thus, according to Marx's sympathetic Russian reviewer,

> According to him, abstract laws do not exist. On the contrary, in his opinion every historical period has laws of its own. . . . In a word, economic life offers us a phenomenon analogous to the history of evolution in other branches of biology. The old economists misunderstood the nature of economic laws when they likened them to the laws of physics and chemistry. A more thorough analysis of phenomena show that social

organisms differ among themselves as fundamentally as plants or animals. [in McClellan, 1977: 419][1]

Elsewhere (1859 Preface to *A Critique of Political Economy;* in McClellan, 1977: 389-390), Marx offers the qualification that the natural science approach applies only to the study of economics:

> A distinction should always be made between the material transformation of the economic conditions of production, which can be determined with the precision of natural science, and the legal, political, religious, aesthetic, or philosophic—in short, ideological forms in which men become conscious of this conflict and fight it out. Just as our opinion of an individual is not based on what he thinks of himself, so can we not judge of such a period of transformation by its own consciousness; on the contrary, this consciousness must be explained rather from the contradictions of material life, from the existing conflict between the social productive forces and the relations of production.

Whatever Marx's expressed self-understanding, I do not believe that he was in practice an empiricist whose theory espoused a rigid determinism that was somehow relaxed only as societies moved from one stage to another. For reasons that shall become apparent, Marx's method differs significantly from the positivistic orientation suggested in these quotations. Marx's methodological self-understanding was limited by his lack of concentrated attention to epistemological issues, as well as by his limited knowledge of the practice of natural science. Marx can hardly be faulted for failing to come to grips with the differing requirements for the study of social and physical phenomena; after all, the great methodological debates within German scholarship occurred almost a half century after the writing of *Capital.*[2]

In *Capital* as well as in his earlier writings, Marx regarded humans as world-producing creatures: That which distinguishes humans from other animals is their ability to erect a project in imagination and subsequently realize it in practice. In achieving their projects humans are constrained by the external conditions they encounter, including the limits of their knowledge; but these conditions—including knowledge—are altered in the very process of realizing the project. As Colletti (1971: 84-85) observes, both causality and teleology are operative in human action: *causality* because within ascertainable limits actions have determinate consequences, and *teleology* because action is consciously goal-oriented and therefore is preceded and partially governed by its intended effects. When Marx writes as a critical philosopher, he is attempting to show how the purposive quality of human activity has been lost as the social world becomes progressively reified in our eyes. At this level of critique, Marx sought to restore our understanding of our potential role as world-creating creatures. But Marx also believes that all actions are not equally effective, that only those governed by a systematic, theoretically guided empirical inquiry are likely to produce the intended results.

Marx's thought thus moves simultaneously on two levels: It formulates the apparent laws of the "natural history" of capitalist economic organization and, at the same time, it demonstrates the ideological (i.e., historically situated) character of those laws so that they might be repealed by self-conscious workers organized collectively in their own interests. Criticism is not enough, nor is a theoretical understanding of how the laws of political economy operate and what they portend for the future of the capitalist economy. Nor is blind struggle sufficient; history does not move automatically toward socialism or any other predetermined end. Early in his writing Marx recognized that both critical awareness and scientific understanding were necessary to guide organized revolutionary activity in order to produce radical social change. Science, criticism, organized class struggle—all are required, as Marx noted in 1843-1844 when he wrote that "the weapon of criticism cannot, of course, supplant the criticism of weapons; material force must be overthrown by material force. But theory, too, will become material force as soon as it seizes the masses" (from the 1843-1844 "Towards a Critique of Hegel's 'Philosophy of Right'"; in McClellan, 1977: 69).

In my view, Marx's *science* must be understood in a restricted sense of that term: His science was not the predictive science of physics or chemistry or biology. The future cannot be predicted; rather, in Sartre's (1971: 115) words, it is "a project to be accomplished." Our knowledge of the future occurs only through activity oriented toward realizing that future; the future itself becomes concrete to us to the extent that we participate and succeed in shaping it. This view is elegantly stated in Sartre's (1971: 115) succinct observation that "what is essential is not that man is made, but that he makes that which made him."

Historical Materialism

As we noted in Chapters 1 and 3, by 1845-1846 Marx had completed a major rethinking of his approach to the study of history, emphasizing the primacy of material conditions in determining the form of social organization, social change, and consciousness itself. In *The German Ideology,* for example, Marx and Engels state that "life is not determined by consciousness, but consciousness by life" (in McClellan, 1977: 164):

The production of ideas, of conceptions, of consciousness, is at first directly interwoven with the material activity and the material intercourse of men, the language of real life. Conceiving, thinking, the mental intercourse of men, appear at this stage as the direct efflux of their material behavior. The same applies to mental production as expressed in the language of politics, laws, morality, religion, metaphysics, etc. of a people. . . .

We set out from real, active men, and on the basis of their real life-process we demonstrate the development of the ideological reflexes and echoes of this life process. [in McClellan, 1977: 164]

This is the fundamental premise of what Marx and Engels were later to term *historical materialism*—the assumption that "material conditions" are fundamental in that they are constitutive of all other aspects of life—social, political, philosophical, ideological, historical. By *material conditions* Marx is referring primarily to what he elsewhere terms the *economic base*—those forces and relations of production whereby human beings produce their means of subsistence. *Forces of production* refers to tools, machinery, and technology in general (including scientific knowledge); *relations of production* signifies the social relations—including those of power and authority—within which the forces of production are institutionalized in a given society. By using phrases such as *direct effluxes* and *ideological reflexes,* Marx appears to be arguing for a simplistic mechanistic determinism—a one-way causality from economic base to social and political institutions, and all forms of consciousness. This is nowhere more succinctly stated than in the oft-cited 1859 preface to *A Critique of Political Economy* (in McClellan, 1977: 389):

In the social production of their life, men enter into definite relations that are indispensable and independent of their will, relations of production which correspond to a definite stage of development of their material productive forces. The sum total of these relations of production constitutes the economic structure of society, the real foundation, on which rises a legal and political superstructure and to which correspond definite forms of social consciousness. The mode of production of material life conditions the social, political, and intellectual life process in general. It is not the consciousness of men that determines their being, but, on the contrary, their social being that determines their consciousness. At a certain stage of their development, the material productive forces of society come in conflict with the existing relations of production, or—what is but a legal expression of the same thing—with the property relations within which they have been at work hitherto. From forms of development of the productive forces these relations turn into their fetters. Then begins an epoch of social revolution. With the change of the economic foundations the entire immense superstructure is more or less rapidly transformed.

Elsewhere—for example, in one celebrated passage on the source of ideas—Marx seems to reduce all consciousness to false ideologies that serve the interest of the wealthy and the powerful:

> The ideas of the ruling class are in every epoch the ruling ideas, i.e., the class which is the ruling material force of society is at the same time its ruling intellectual force. . . . The ruling ideas are nothing more than the ideal expression of the dominant material relationships. [in McClellan, 1977: 176]

Taken at face value, this position would seem to argue that ideas directly reflect material conditions, making it highly unlikely that contradictory ideas would ever develop—a conclusion that Marx hardly draws. In fact, Marx hedges his bets. In the following description of his overall approach, Marx first asserts the fundamental importance of material conditions on society, the state, and consciousness; he then qualifies this assertion to allow for reciprocal causation:

> This conception of history depends on our ability to expound the real process of production, starting out from the material production of life itself, and to comprehend the form of intercourse connected with this and created by this mode of production (i.e., civil society in various stages) as the basis of all history; and to show its association as State, to explain all the different theoretical products and forms of consciousness, religion, philosophy, ethics, etc. etc. and trace their origin from that basis; by which means, of course, the whole thing can be depicted in its totality (*and therefore, too, the reciprocal action of these various sides on one another*). [in McClellan, 1977: 172; emphasis added]

While Marx sees material conditions as highly determinate of all other aspects of social life, he stops short of simple unilinear causality, alluding to a more systematic notion of reciprocal causation with the economic base as somehow primary in importance. Marx never attempted to work out the implications of this position, a deficiency that has permitted much acrimonious disagreement among those who feel that loyalty to Marx's word is an important ingredient of social theory. While it is certainly possibly to read passages such as these as evidence for a "reflection theory"[3] of history, to obtain a real understanding of the complexity of Marx's thinking one must not look to programmatic passages such as these, but to the actual working-out of his economic theory (primarily in *Capital* and *Grundrisse*), and to his political essays. The implications of this materialist view of history are traced out elsewhere in *The German Ideology.* For one thing, in Marx's view it spells the end to speculation, the death of philosophy "as an independent branch of knowledge":

> Where speculation ends—in real life—there real, positive science begins: the representation of the practical activity, of the practical process of development of men. Empty talk about consciousness ceases, and real knowledge has to take its place. [in McClellan, 1977: 165]

> Every profound philosophical problem is resolved ... quite simply into an empirical fact. [in McClellan, 1977: 174]

Among the complex philosophical issues resolved into "empirical facts" by this "real, positive science" is the matter of human essence (Feuerbach's species-being), which Marx now regards in purely socio-logical terms:[4]

> What they [individuals] are, therefore, coincides with their production, both with what they produce and with how they produce. The nature of individuals thus depends on the material conditions determining their production. [in McClellan, 1977: 161]

> This sum of productive forces, capital funds, and social forms of intercourse, which every individual and generation finds in existence as something given, is the real basis of what the philosophers have conceived as "substance" and "essence of man." [in McClellan, 1977: 173]

Human nature is thus sociologically constituted in the forces and relations of production, which are themselves historically given, at least in the short run. In Marx's view of history, the forces of production may gradually change as science and technology evolve, but the relations of production are much more rigid, serving as an "integuement" that binds the forces of production into a relatively small number of different socioeconomic types that Marx refers to as "modes of production." Each mode of production is characterized by the dominance of a specific productive force, and by a set of social relations that serve initially to develop that force. Principal among these relations are property[5] relations, giving rise to social classes. For any given mode of production there are two primary[6] classes, based on the principal type of property that predominates in subsistence production: One class will control access to (and sometimes ownership of) that property, while the other's labor will be used to produce wealth from that property. Thus, in any mode of production, one type of property will be of decisive importance in determining the predominant class relations in a two-class model.

In *The German Ideology,* Marx identifies five different stages or modes of production that, in his view at the time, all societies have traversed:[7]

- tribal ownership (primitive communism), characterized initially by nomadic hunting and gathering, with the relative absence of private property (except for stone hand tools), and a correspondingly highly rudimentary division of labor; this phase ends with the development of settled agriculture, the production of an economic surplus, and the emergence of private property and class structure
- classical slavery, with the principal form of property being slaves and the tools they use to operate the mines and farm the lands, and with slaveowners and slaves being the two chief classes
- feudalism, in which land serves as the principal form of property, with landlords and serfs (landless peasants legally tied to the property they work for the benefit of the landlord) the two predominant classes
- capitalism, in which machinery (capital) is the principal form of property, with capitalists (Marx uses *bourgeoisie* interchangeably) and proletarians (workers) the two dominant classes
- communism, in which both property and class are abolished, since all of society will hold communal title to the principal means of production

With communism this historical process comes to an end, since the principal sources of conflict—differential class ownership of private property—presumably no longer exists.

Marx adheres to a sort of cultural lag (Ogburn, 1964) theory of history, whereby socioeconomic relations emerge alongside new forces of production, but thereafter solidify in order to serve the interests of the dominant class. After a point, the very social relations that once served to foment growth in the forces of production come to act as constraints upon further development. At this point only revolution can break them apart and permit further growth to occur:

> In the development of the productive forces there comes a stage when productive forces and means of intercourse are brought into being that, under the existing relationships, only cause mischief, and are no longer productive but destructive forces. [*The German Ideology;* in McClellan, 1977: 179]

Or, in the more dramatic language of the polemical *Communist Manifesto* (published two years later), where Marx draws parallels between the demise of feudalism and the projected demise of capitalism:

> At a certain stage in the development of these means of production and of exchange, the conditions under which feudal society produced and exchanged . . . in one word, the feudal relations of property become no longer compatible with the already developed productive forces; they

become so many fetters. They had to be burst asunder; they were burst asunder. . . .

A similar movement is going on before our own eyes. . . . The productive forces at the disposal of [bourgeois] society no longer tend to further the development of the conditions of bourgeois property; on the contrary, they have become too powerful for these conditions, by which they are fettered, and so soon as they overcome these fetters, they bring disorder into the whole of bourgeois society, endanger the existence of bourgeois property. . . .

The weapons with which the bourgeoisie felled feudalism to the ground are now turned against the bourgeoisie itself. [in McClellan, 1977: 225-226]

Social change is thus violent and abrupt, and is engineered by the social class that will become dominant in the succeeding stage. Thus, for example, "from the serfs of the Middle Ages sprang the chartered burghers of the earliest towns. From these burgesses the first elements of the bourgeoisie were developed" (*Communist Manifesto;* in McClellan, 1977: 222). And, in a parallel fashion, the proletariat of the capitalist mode of production are seen as the key to the communist society of the future, since it is the first social class whose economic function is highly strategic:

A class is called forth, which has to bear all the burdens of society without enjoying its advantages, which, when ousted from society, is forced into the most decided antagonism to all other classes; a class which forms the majority of all members of society, and from which emanates the consciousness of the necessity of a fundamental revolution, the communist consciousness. . . . In all revolutions until now the mode of activity always remained unscathed and it was only a question of a different distribution of this activity. [*The German Ideology;* in McClellan, 1977: 179]

The motive force for the proletariat to act is simple: growing poverty. Revolution occurs not because of subjective alienation, but because capitalism has simultaneously produced grinding poverty alongside the technological means of abolishing it:

This "alienation" (to use a term which will be comprehensible to the philosophers) can, of course, only be abolished given two practical premises. For it to become an "intolerable" power, i.e., a power against which men make a revolution, it must necessarily have rendered the great mass of humanity "propertyless," and produced, at the same time, the contradiction of an existing world of wealth and culture . . . and furthermore, because only with this universal development of productive forces is a universal intercourse between men established, which produces in all nations simultaneously the phenomenon of the "propertyless man"

... makes each nation dependent on the revolutions of the others, and finally has put world-historical, empirically universal individuals in place of local ones. [*The German Ideology;* in McClellan, 1977: 170-171]

Although Marx believes himself to be proceeding "scientifically," it should be noted that his method at this stage would hardly satisfy modern canons of scientific analysis. *The German Ideology* develops its central concepts out of a confrontation with other ideas, not from a sustained and systematic effort to ground theory in empirical research. It remains, in other words, largely an exercise in critique, although one devoted to asserting the importance of empirical inquiry over critique. Marx's review of economic and social history is at best anecdotal and superficial, a highly simplistic account where it is not simply wrong. His assertion of the eventual ascendance of the proletariat—first announced in his *Critique of Hegel's Philosophy of Right* in 1844[8]—is a logical derivative of his theory of history, rather than the result of a study of (for example) European social movements. The logic is simple and therefore appealing. In a two-class model in which the numerically inferior class becomes progressively wealthy as a necessary consequence of the impoverishment of the more numerous class, revolution would appear to be its only hope of redress. When the dominated class constitutes the overwhelming mass of society—its principal productive resource—this will necessarily result in radical socioeconomic changes.

Had Marx ended his argument with *The German Ideology* or the *Communist Manifesto,* its obvious polemical power would have lacked any credible claim to scientific grounding. Whether or not this would have weakened its impact is an interesting topic for speculation. But, in fact, he did not stop with logic and anecdote: He eventually folded his compelling vision of history into an equally compelling analysis of instability in the capitalist economy. This analysis, which sought to demonstrate how recurrent economic crises are part of the very structure of capitalist economic relations, wedded a logical and systematic theory to an exhaustive study of the British economy. If Marx retained his vision of social change, it was eventually moderated through an economic theory that sought its legitimacy on scientific, rather than philosophical, grounds. It is to this theory that we now turn, particularly as it was most fully developed in *Capital.*

THE "LAWS OF MOTION" OF CAPITALIST PRODUCTION

Marx himself distinguished natural from social history when he echoed Vico in observing that "human history differs from natural history in this, that we have made the former, but not the latter" (*Capital: Volume I,* 1967: 372, footnote). Later in the same comment, Marx contends that the "abstract materialism of natural science . . . excludes history and its process"; this he regarded as a "weak point" that becomes evident whenever natural scientists "venture beyond the bounds of their own specialty" (p. 373). Human history, for Marx, thus has a double nature: It is at once project and constraint, the result and source of human activity. The Marxist concept of praxis captures this mutual transformation of subject and object; a self-conscious praxis is the way in which people can hope to reappropriate the social dimension of what has become a naturalized human history. In order to better understand how this is so, we shall turn to an analysis of Marx's theory of capitalist production. By laying out the nature of both law and agency in *Capital,* I hope to show how Marx's "science" must be filtered through his enduring philosophical commitment to the power of a transformative praxis.

The first volume of *Capital* sets up a highly simplified model of capitalist economic production, based on Marx's analysis of conditions in Britain, at the time capitalism's most advanced economy. By simplifying the interrelated processes of production, distribution, exchange, and consumption to their essential elements, Marx hoped to reveal laws that operate as structural tendencies within the givens of the capitalist economy: production for the sake of privately appropriated profit rather than social welfare. By *structural tendencies* I mean forces that result from structural characteristics of the economic system, creating pressures within that system for particular sorts of actions. The working-out of these tendencies will depend on concrete circumstances, including (and especially) the responses of the key groups of actors involved. Actions are not predictable, nor are their concrete results. Only the long-term structural conditions that create the need and opportunity for action can be anticipated in advance, and then only in the broadest terms possible—for example, knowing that an upturn in the business cycle will eventually be followed by a downward swing.

Marx lays out the basic framework of his analysis in Volume I of *Capital,* which he then fleshes out in later volumes, particularly the more concrete analysis of Volume III. The key tendencies analyzed by Marx in *Capital* are those which contribute to economic instability. These give rise to various types of economic crises—some cyclical, in Marx's view, and some chronic. Crises, in turn, provide the framework within which the central dynamic for social change operates—the struggle between wage-labor and capital. As we shall see, the demise of capitalism is not as inevitable as a reading of the *Communist Manifesto* might suggest.

Economic Concepts and Political Struggle

Capital begins with a discussion of the commodity—the logical starting-point, since it is closest to everyday experience, a familiar feature of capitalism, therefore, and likely to be reified in our minds as a perfectly natural, taken-for-granted "thing." As we saw in Chapter 4, however, Marx regards the commodity as the fetishized manifestation of hidden social relationships that alone make its existence intelligible. Using the commodity, seemingly "an object outside us" (*Capital: Volume I;* in McClellan, 1977: 421), Marx hopes to unravel and then reconstruct the political economy of capitalism. He begins with a discussion of the twofold value of the commodity—its utility as an object of consumption, and the value it brings in exchange. Why is the value of an object measured by its price? Classical political economy had recognized that the utility or *use-value* of a commodity was not necessarily the same as its *exchange-value,* but chose to ignore the difference and focus on the latter—measured by price—as the measure of an object's worth. After all, utility is subjective and probably unmeasurable; the price of an object is a datum known to everyone. Marx argued that this self-evident equation was in fact historically rooted—that only under an economic system where everything had its price could one forget that price is not necessarily the measure of value.

Marx then seeks to explain how exchange-value governs the relationship between commodities, and in particular the underlying social relationships that determine the rate at which different commodities exchange. In Hegelian terms, one might say that the commodity-form is the surface appearance of some deeper, underlying reality; Marx's task is to penetrate through the appearance to that reality. The key, for Marx, is the labor process—the social relationships that constitute the reality of capitalism and determine the rates at which commodities exchange. The key to the identification of use-value with exchange-value is therefore to be sought in the labor process.

One of the distinguishing features of capitalism is that labor is also a commodity—it can be bought and sold for a price. Like all commodities, therefore, labor possesses both use-value and exchange-value—and, as with all commodities, we falsely tend to equate the two. The use-value of labor, according to Marx, is its ability to create new value where none previously existed—to convert matter to forms that are useful for human beings. Only human labor is capable of doing this—of recognizing the potential utility in an object, devising the techniques and tools necessary to realize that potential, and then setting the necessary machinery in motion. The exchange-value of labor, on the other hand, is simply the power of labor to produce commodities—energy that can be drawn upon to produce goods and services. One of Marx's key distinctions is therefore between *labor* as value, and *labor power* as productive energy.[9] Under capitalism we lose sight of the former, and are left only with the exchange value of labor—as measured by its wage. Furthermore, just as labor understood as value is unique, reflecting the creative potential of each individual, so labor understood as exchange is highly general: Each unique feature of labor is stripped away as all labor-power is reduced to its simplest, most deskilled, and hence most exchangeable form. Marx says that labor in exchange comes to be increasingly *abstract* under capitalism—that is, reduced to its most common denominator.

As we saw in Chapter 3, Marx adhered to the *labor theory of value*—the belief that the exchange value of a commodity is a function of the amount of labor-time required to produce it. Commodities exchange in proportion to the relative amounts of labor required to produce them. If we regard societies as having a certain amount of labor power given to the production of commodities, then we can begin to formulate laws that govern the exchange of those commodities and the allocation of labor necessary to produce them. To take a simple model, supposing it takes six hours to make a pair of shoes, while it requires three hours to make a belt. Then, according to the above reasoning, a pair of shoes should exchange for two belts. Why? Because if a pair of shoes bought only one belt, it would hardly be worthwhile for anyone to make shoes; one could expend half the time making a belt, while realizing the same rate of return. So shoemakers would become beltmakers, shoes would become scarcer, and their price would rise until it again became worthwhile to make shoes. Conversely, if a scarcity in shoes resulted in a high rate of exchange—say three belts for a pair of shoes—then shoe production would become highly desirable; after all, six hours of labor in shoe production would exchange for three belts, representing nine hours of labor in belt manufacture. Belt makers would be wise to shift into shoe manufacture, since they could make an equivalent return with less time. Such a shift, however, would result in overproduction of shoes, depressing their exchange-value. As before, the exchange-value of shoes would drop until equilibrium is again restored. *Long-run equilibrium, according to the labor theory of value, is the exchange rate at which equivalent quantities of labor-time are exchanged.* Such exchanges need not be direct, of course; in reality, both will exchange for money, which becomes the universal medium of exchange.

This simple model makes several key assumptions about how the economy operates. First, it assumes that all labor is commensurable—for example, that the labor required for complex manufacturing processes is comparable with the simplest deskilled labor, and so that when one seeks to exchange belts for shoes, one can directly compare the labor that went into producing each. By referring to *socially necessary labor-time,* Marx is emphasizing this common quality of labor that he believed obtained under the average production conditions in society. Marx believed that commensurability was a reasonable assumption for at least two reasons. First, under industrial capitalism labor becomes increasingly deskilled, so that in the long run all forms of labor become substitutable for one another: Factory work is reduced to uniform detail labor. In the context of the emerging industrial capitalism of the mid-nineteenth century in particular, such an assumption would easily seem warranted, inasmuch as automation promised to reduce human labor to the simplest of tasks. Second, complex or skilled labor can be understood as a multiple of simple labor, with the multiplier being the cost (again, in labor-time) of producing the skilled labor. In other words, since labor is itself a commodity, its exchange value (its wage) will reflect its own cost of production—which includes not only food, shelter, and other subsistence costs, but training costs as well. A computer programmer, for example, will exchange for a wage many times higher than the operatives who produce electronic circuitry on the assembly line; but then it has presumably taken proportionately longer to train the programmer.

The second assumption Marx makes is that labor and capital are mobile,[10] and that, therefore, in the long run, supply and demand will equilibrate at the cost of production (measured in terms of labor-time). We saw this in the example of shoes and belts: Any failure to exchange in proportion to their relative amounts of labor-time triggers a shift in production between the two activities, which in the long run produces the equilibrium exchange. *It is important to recognize that Marx's approach is based on long-term costs of production, and not on short-term variations in supply and demand.* In the language of contemporary economics, Marx's model is a production-function model based on the supply-side alone. In focusing on long-term production costs rather than short-term supply-and-demand adjustments, Marx hopes to gain an understanding of the allocation of aggregated production decisions across various sectors of the economy (he calls these "departments"). Such a long-term understanding of macrolevel economic forces is bought at the expense of understanding the shorter-term microeconomic behavior of individual firms. Marx is more than willing to pay this price, since he refuses to regard demand as a causally independent variable in determining exchange. This is because demand is itself produced under capitalism—both directly, through the manipulation of consumer wants, and indirectly, through the generation of income inequality. The latter in particular, as we shall see, plays a key role in determining long-term trends in the rate of profit and hence systemwide economic health.

The key to understanding the dynamics of capitalist production is *surplus value,* the discovery and analysis of which Marx and Engels regarded as their greatest achievement. As we noted in Chapter 3, surplus value is the additional value[11] produced by labor beyond the cost of reproducing the labor itself. I noted above that labor, like any commodity, has a cost of production—the value of the goods and services that enable labor to subsist and reproduce itself. This value is, of course, variable across time and place: The definition of *subsistence* or *working wage* is culturally bound, subject to workers' expectations, and a principal object of the struggle between labor and capital. But whatever the exchange value of labor, if it is possible to employ wage-labor for a longer time period than is necessary to produce that value, then the additional period of employment produces a surplus value that is the capitalists' to dispose.

Under the feudal economy that preceded capitalism in Europe, the production of surplus value was obvious. Serfs spent a certain amount of time working their landlord's fields, and it was clear to all that this surplus portion of their labor-time was at his disposal. The production of surplus value under capitalism differs significantly, however, in that it is invisible: Workers do not divide their workday into two parts, one of which is spent in the capitalist's part of the factory and the other in their own. Rather, they work an undivided day, for which they are paid less than the value of the goods they produce. If one imagines capitalist society to be a single large factory producing all the goods required for society's subsistence, the workers in the factory will produce goods in excess of their own subsistence requirements; the value of those excess goods constitutes their surplus value production. Since accounts are not kept in this fashion, however, the surplus is not readily evident under capitalist production; in fact, the existence of a surplus is not even acknowledged. A didactic reason for Marx's use of the concept, then, is to urge workers to see their key role in producing value. This contradicts the prevailing view—sanctified by conventional economic theory—that capital and land, as well as labor, are themselves sources of value. Rather, Marx argues, *everything* of value is produced by human labor; only ideological mystification prevents workers from recognizing their role in producing not only their own subsistence requirements, but an additional surplus that is appropriated by landlords and capitalists in the form of rents and profits. As with many of Marx's central concepts, the notion of surplus thus plays a dual role within Marxist theory: an economic role (the source of profit) and a critical role (in dereifying the false assumption that workers are being paid the full value of their labor-time).[12]

Marx analyzed the value of commodity production in terms of three key elements, given in equation 1:[13]

$$\text{value} = C + V + S \tag{1}$$

C or *constant capital* is the value of the means of production used up during the production process—primarily the depreciated value of machines, buildings, and raw materials. It is what we ordinarily think of as "capital" in factory production. Marx regards constant capital as the congealed labor of past generations of workers. V, or *variable capital,* on the other hand, is the value of the labor-power that sets production in motion, represented by the wage bill. It represents the cost of producing and reproducing the work force. It is interesting to note that Marx regards labor as variable capital—capital because workers are increasingly reduced to the status of appendages to machines, variable because they can be brought in and cast off according to the requirements of production. Finally, S or *surplus value,* as we have seen, is the value of unpaid labor-time appropriated by the capitalist during the production process—workers' unpaid labor-time beyond that which is "socially necessary" to sustain the standard of living of the working class. Surplus value is the key to capitalist economic production, for it is the source of all profits, including those that are accumulated and reinvested in enhanced productive capacity.

Marx defines the rate of surplus value (S') as the ratio of unpaid to paid labor-time, or

$$S' = S/V \tag{2}$$

In Marx's theory this measure plays a dual role—it is an important constituent of the rate of profit, while at the same time it also serves the didactic function of revealing the degree of worker exploitation. The rate of surplus value is thus at once an economic index and a measure of the rate of exploitation, and in the latter sense can be used to educate workers concerning the degree to which their labor power is alienated. For example, if the socially necessary labor-time (V) required to produce a day's subsistence is 8 hours and workers remain in the factory

12 hours, then the 4 hours of surplus (S) yields a rate of exploitation of 50%: Workers are laboring half as much again for the capitalist as for themselves. S therefore calls attention to the political class struggle, and in Volume I, Parts III and IV of *Capital* Marx documents the historical struggle over the size and disposition of the surplus during the recent history of British capitalism. He first looks at what he terms *absolute surplus value*—the surplus that depends upon the length of the working day, which constituted the locus of the earliest struggles between labor and capital. As the working day was shortened, however, this fight shifted to the intensity of exploitation—a "closer filling up of the pores of the working day . . . this condensation of a greater mass of labor into a given period" (*Capital: Volume I*, 1967: 410). Such intensification of the labor process is achieved by assembly line speed-up, shorter work breaks, and the overall rationalization of the labor process that was to achieve its full fruition at the turn of the century in Taylor's "scientific management" theories. Marx terms the surplus value produced by such intensification *relative.*

The rate of exploitation given in equation 2 is thus a function of both absolute and relative surplus value, which together determine the numerator of the ratio (S). It is also a function of variable capital (V), the denominator. One way of increasing the rate of surplus value extraction is to cheapen the cost of reproducing the work force. This can be achieved by two principal methods: either forcing the workers to do with less, thereby lowering their standard of living, or else by lowering their cost of living. While both strategies have been used historically, the latter is likely to be more politically viable, particularly once the working class has achieved a degree of organization and power. There are many ways the workers' living costs can be lowered, including providing company housing with controlled rents,[14] importing cheaper foreign goods, and mass producing cheap domestic products.[15]

It is important to note that the rate of exploitation is treated by Marx as dependent first and foremost on the relative strength of workers and capitalists. As with all of Marx's key variables, S and V are not data that are somehow "given," the familiar *ceteris paribus* of economic theory. Rather, they are both input and output of the economic system under analysis: *input* in that, for a given level of S and V, the rate of surplus value extraction (as we shall see) will partially determine profitability and hence overall economic performance, but also *output* in that S and V themselves are constantly changing as a result of economic performance and the corresponding degree of worker organization. In my view, there are very few "givens" or predictable outcomes in Marx's theory of capitalist development: Everything depends on the interaction between politics and economics, and Marx's fundamental variables are constituted politically as well as economically.

Marx's Crisis Theory

To better understand this point, let us look at Marx's theory of crisis in capitalist economies. He begins by noting a strong structural tendency toward automation. During the period of competitive capitalism (with which Marx was primarily concerned), individual capitalists were under continual economic pressure to increase the efficiency of production—to produce commodities at lower unit costs in order to remain competitive. While this could be achieved by economizing on either of the two principal component costs of production—constant or variable capital—Marx believed that in the long run the key to lowering production costs was mechanization, which meant increasing C relative to V. Thus, driven by the economic imperative to undersell competitors in order to survive, individual capitalists would be forced to substitute increasingly efficient machines for human labor. Throughout the economy, therefore, there is a long-run tendency toward mechanization, making it possible for the remaining workers to produce ever-larger quantities of goods with ever-decreasing labor-time. Marx termed the degree of mechanization the *organic composition of capital,* and denoted it by the symbol Q, representing the ratio of constant to total (constant plus variable) capital:[16]

$$Q = C/(C + V) \qquad [3]$$

As with equation 2, the constituent variables that determine Q in equation 3 must be understood politically as well as economically. V, as we have seen, reflects the struggle over labor's living standards as well as efforts to reduce the cost of living for workers. C reflects the amount of past capital accumulation, hence the extent to which capital has previously succeeded in mechanizing the production process. Because one purpose of mechanization is to increase labor productivity,[17] as the organic composition of capital rises there is a tendency for the rate of surplus value to rise as well: As C increases relative to V, S also increases relative to V. So C, V, and S are all interdependent on one another. Together, they determine the rate of profit, defined by Marx as the ratio of surplus value to total capital advanced, or

$$P = S/(C + V) \qquad [4]$$

It follows algebraically that the rate of profit can be decomposed into two terms, consisting of the rate of surplus value and the organic composition of capital:

$$P = S'*(1 - Q) \qquad [5]$$

where S' is given by equation 2 and Q is given by equation 3.[18]

We are now ready to analyze the dynamics of capitalist production in terms of C, V, and S, indicating how structured instability is a necessary feature of the capitalist economic system. It should be born in mind that, according to Marx, in order to remain competitive capitalists must continually revolutionize their production methods, cutting costs and increasing labor productivity. The surplus, in other words, must constantly be maximized and invested in further growth—not because the capitalists are necessarily greedy or avaricious, but because their very survival as capitalists depends upon it. Marx therefore argued that a rising organic composition was the hallmark of capitalist production (1967: 449) which tends to undermine the stability of the system itself.

There are various types of crises that can be identified in Marx's writings.[19] Following Sweezy (1942), we will divide these into two broad classes: profitability crises, which result from both long- and short-term structural constraints on the ability of capitalists to make sufficient profits so that continued production is worthwhile; and realization crises, which result from the inability of capitalists to sell the goods they have already produced.[20] Each type of crisis, as we shall see, has an affinity for a particular form of political strategy and practice.

Profitability Crises

Marx assumes that a certain minimal level of profitability is necessary for capitalists in a given industry to be willing to reinvest their earnings in further accumulation. Once the rate of profit drops below this expected level, investment will be shifted to other industrial sectors. Should the generalized rate of profit throughout the economy drop, productive investment will be curtailed altogether, with capitalists shifting their funds into more liquid assets, or out of the national economy. When this occurs, production stagnates and a generalized economic crisis occurs. Marx analyzed two classes of profitability crises: short-term fluctuations of the business cycle, which he believed would eventually amplify into powerfully disruptive economic depressions; and a long-term trend toward protracted profit stagnation that could eventually prove fatal to the economy as a whole. Let us consider both of these in turn.

Crises of the business cycle: As we have noted, capitalists who fail to accumulate, reinvest, and grow are doomed to competitive failure. Growth is thus structurally embedded in competitive capitalist economic production. But growth increases the demand for labor, the increasing scarcity of which results in higher wages. At some point these rising wages begin to cut into profits, dampening further growth. The classical economists were aware of this problem, and offered a solution: the Malthusian hypothesis that relatively prosperous workers would experience lower morbidity and mortality, thereby increasing in numbers with a concomitant depressing effect on wages. Marx rejected such external correctives, arguing instead that the economy contains its own in-built corrective mechanism in the form of the labor pool of unemployed workers—the so-called reserve army of labor, the function of which is to keep wages depressed. Under ordinary circumstances, Marx reasoned, there is a large pool of marginal workers who compete with one another for jobs, assuring that wages will be kept at subsistence levels.[21] This pool includes workers who have lost their jobs as a result of growth and contraction throughout the economy, migrant labor and minorities generally, young people, and often women. During a period of economic growth this pool will be drawn from until it diminishes to a point where it no longer serves to curb wage demands. If the growth phase is long or strong enough, increasingly scarce workers will be able to organize effectively, utilizing their scarcity as leverage in demanding better working conditions and higher pay. As such concessions are granted, profits begin to suffer.[22] Accumulation slows, and growth is curbed—initially in the industry where growth has been the strongest, then in related industries. When profits fall below a certain level of expectation, capitalists shift their investment elsewhere, and a period of stagnation ensues. The extent of the stagnation will initially depend on the extent to which the affected industries are central to the economy, but as workers are laid off—reducing the demand for goods that are being produced in other economic sectors—the stagnation becomes general. Flagging demand exacerbates the crisis, and reinvestment all but ceases. A period of economic decline now ensues. Factories close down, inventories mount, and the credit system is shaken as loans go unpaid. The reserve army of labor, formerly depleted, is rapidly replenished with the growing ranks of the unemployed. Labor goes from scarcity to abundance, and wages sink accordingly. The decline in wages begins to restore the conditions of profitability that existed prior to the growth phase, and capitalists again reinvest.[23] The period of economic decline bottoms out, and growth resumes.

Marx sought to demonstrate in *Capital* that these alternate cycles of boom and bust lasted about 10 years. He does not regard them as merely recurrent fluctuations, however, but rather as waves that are amplified with each new cycle. The peaks get higher and the troughs lower, until eventually a crisis occurs that threatens the foundations of the system itself. This is because the business cycle is seen as contributing to the growth in economic concentration and centralized control that Marx regards as a central feature of capitalism. We have previously noted a long-term tendency for the organic composition of capital to grow: Large, capital-intensive factories tend to replace smaller, more labor-intensive ones as a result of the demands of competitive survival. This tendency is abetted by the business cycle. With each downward phase, the less competitive businesses fail and are absorbed by the more successful ones. The big firms cannibalize the smaller, until eventually— as the cycles grow more and more severe—only the very largest remain. These are extremely susceptible to future fluctuations, since they have large masses of capital equipment and inventory tied up in production, and therefore cannot satisfactorily adjust to economic downswings by simply laying off workers. The economy becomes brittle. A life-threatening crisis will eventually occur. Whether capitalism itself perishes will depend on concrete circumstances, in particular the strength of the working class.

Cyclical crises create an opportunity for political organizing, since with each downswing capitalism's promise of continuous growth is proven to be false. As the crises worsen, more and more workers are adversely affected, and the possibilities for a revolutionary working-class movement (in Marx's view) grow. At the same time, downswings are interspersed with growth spurts during which unemployment falls, wages rise, and segments of the work force experience the promise of prosperity. This helps to legitimate the economic system, while providing breathing space for capitalists to effect reforms in hopes of dampening or even averting the next cycle. Thus cyclical crises are by nature somewhat open-ended or indeterminate. They would seem to call for a political strategy that takes advantage of each downswing, building a solid revolutionary base while seeking to convince a growing body of workers that capitalists' efforts at repair and reform are doomed to repeated failure. In other words, Marx's theory of the business cycle has an affinity for the politics of class struggle, since without a powerful and organized working class there is no guarantee that some inevitable crisis will bring the system to collapse.

Crises resulting from long-term profit stagnation: Overlaid on his theory of the business cycle, Marx also has a theory of a long-term tendency for the overall rate of profit to decline to critically low levels.

To the extent that this theory is correct, it implies that capitalism is in the long run doomed, even if it is able to surmount the periodic crises associated with the business cycle. For this reason Marx's theory of the declining rate of profit has proven appealing to those Marxists who prefer to view the demise of capitalism as inevitable.

We noted previously that in equation 3 there is a long-run tendency for the organic composition of capital to rise. As the capitalist seeks to maximize profits through the production of absolute and relative surplus value, V will decline relative to C, and Q will therefore rise. But at the same time, as V becomes very small relative to C, the organic composition (Q) approaches unity, and the term $(1 - Q)$ in equation 5 must therefore approach 0. Since the rate of profit (P) is the product of 1 $- Q$ with S', if this term reaches 0 so must the rate of profit. On the other hand, inasmuch as the reason for mechanization in the first place is to increase surplus value, the downward pressure on profitability resulting from rising Q will to a greater or lesser extent be offset by a rising S', rendering P unpredictable. This increase in S' can be achieved by increasing S, particularly in its relative surplus value form; by decreasing V, by either importing cheap foreign goods or utilizing cheap foreign labor directly; and by means of the reserve army of the unemployed, which enables capitalists to reduce wages to subsistence levels or lower for periods of time. Alternatively, the rate of increase in Q may be partly mitigated by new technologies that reduce the cost of capital as well as labor, or by the importation of cheap foreign raw materials and capital.

Marx was aware of these considerations, but argued on logical grounds that as the organic composition reaches a high level, additional increases in productivity (hence S') are inadequate as a strategy to maintain profitability (*Capital,* Volume 3: 247).[24] The profit-maximizing strategy of individual capitalists will then result in a profitability crisis for the economy as a whole. Marx thus regards chronic stagnation as a structural imperative of capitalist economic production, although its actual working-out will depend on concrete historical circumstances.

In my view, Marx offers the declining rate of profit as a tendency the outcome of which depends on a variety of empirical conditions, rather than a universal law leading to inevitable economic collapse.[25] During the early part of the twentieth century, however, many key socialist activists believed that the theory of the declining rate of profit was Marx's singular contribution to understanding the crises of capitalism, and that in fact it operated as a law that spelled out capitalism's inevitable demise. The German Social Democrat Karl Kautsky, for example, called for a politics of "actionless waiting" on the grounds that the predicted collapse was soon to come. If one believes that an event is destined to occur, there is little that concerted action can do except perhaps to hasten the inevitable. A theory of crisis based on the inevitable decline of the rate of profit would seem to have an affinity for a political practice that is largely passive, rather than for an active class struggle that seeks to take advantage of each opening while it exists.

Realization Crises

As noted above, realization crises result from the capitalists' inability to realize the value of goods already produced. As demand falls and sales decline, capitalists are left with growing inventories the prices of which fall below their production cost. As with profitability crises, realization crises can be categorized into two distinct types.

Realization crises resulting from underconsumption: The most significant realization crises are due to underconsumption on the part of workers, whose progressive impoverishment renders them unable to afford the goods that they are themselves producing. This impoverishment has both short- and long-term aspects. In the short term, during the recessionary trough of the business cycle, unemployment rises and aggregate demand falls. This exacerbates the recession, resulting in still greater unemployment and even lowered demand, in a self-reinforcing cycle that is corrected only when wages drop sufficiently to restore profitability. But in the long term this strategy is destructive for the capitalist system as a whole: It only can portend chronically flagging demand, since ultimately the masses of workers constitute the principal market for consumer goods. In other words, the short-term production requirements confronted by individual capitalists, which call for cutting labor costs in order to maintain profitability, conflict with the long-term system need for a strong consumer goods market. Under capitalism, goods must not only be produced, they must also be purchased, if the value tied up in them is to be realized. According to Marx, production and consumption requirements are thus in direct contradiction with one another: The rationally acting, utility-maximizing individual capitalist must necessarily be concerned with the former, although this denies the system as a whole the level of consumption it needs for sustained economic viability.[26]

As is well known, Marx believed that workers become increasingly impoverished as capitalism develops—not only relative to capitalists,[27] but in absolute terms as well.

> The modern labourer . . . instead of rising with the progress of industry, sinks deeper and deeper below the conditions of existence of his own class. He becomes a pauper, and pauperism develops more rapidly than

population and wealth. [from the *Communist Manifesto,* in McClellan, 1977: 230]

The same causes which develop the expansive power of capital also develop the labour power at its disposal. The relative mass of the industrial reserve army therefore increases with the potential energy of wealth. But the greater this reserve army in proportion to the active labour-army, the greater is the mass of consolidated surplus population, whose misery is in inverse ratio to its torment of labor. The more extensive, finally, the lazarus-layers of the working-class, and the industrial reserve army, the greater is official pauperism. This is the absolute general law of capitalist accumulation. [from *Capital: Volume I;* in McClellan, 1977: 482]

Furthermore, the size of the working class increases, swollen by "the lower strata of the middle class—the small tradespeople, shopkeepers, and retired tradesmen generally, the handicraftmen and peasants" (*Communist Manifesto;* in McClellan, 1977: 227)—not to mention "entire sections of the ruling class" who succumb to industrial competition (p. 229). Thus, according to Marx, there is a tendency for a two-class society to emerge, the capitalist class getting smaller and wealthier, the working class getting more numerous and more impoverished. These forces all contribute to a long-term tendency toward declining demand, at the same time that capitalism develops its productive forces, unleashing an historically unprecedented torrent of goods. Capitalism, Marx points out, is the first economic system to suffer from chronic overproduction—from glut.

Other factors, of course, may intervene to amplify or dampen these tendencies: As Marx notes in connection with the "absolute general law of capitalist accumulation," "like all other laws it is modified in its working by many circumstances, the analysis of which does not concern us here" (from *Capital: Volume I;* in McClellan, 1977: 482). There are a number of counteracting forces:[28]

- the creation of new industries that create a demand for labor, thereby raising wages and hence aggregate demand (this is more likely to happen during the earlier stages of industrialization, rather than the latter)
- rapid population growth, which creates new markets while at the same time depressing wages and thereby enhancing profitability, accumulation, and further growth
- expansion of sales into foreign markets, since a sufficient mass of foreign consumers can counteract sluggish demand at home
- capital export, which can cheapen the cost of production and hence render commodities affordable even in the face of sluggish wages at home

- consumption on the part of workers whose income does not derive from commodity production, and hence whose wages need not be depressed to maintain profitability (these include the landed gentry and *rentiers* in general, middlemen and merchants, salespeople and advertisers, and service workers in general)
- public expenditures of various sorts

The latter have proven especially important in counteracting underconsumption, especially in the modern welfare state. Anticipating Keynesian economics by almost three-quarters of a century, Marx recognized that government would play a key role in shoring up flagging demand. This could occur in a variety of ways: by means of direct state expenditures on capital projects, from dams to defense; by means of income transfers to the poor, which serve to maintain at least a minimal level of consumption among the masses; and by means of direct state consumption, through vastly expanded public sector employment. These activities are not without their own adverse consequences, of course. To the extent that state expenditures are financed out of current taxation, they must be paid for by either workers or capitalists. The former reduces V, thereby exacerbating the decline in aggregate demand; the latter reduces S, lowering profitability and hence discouraging necessary capital accumulation. On the other hand, if state expenditures are financed through the issuance of debt instruments—which occurs when public expenditures exceed revenues—then consumption is bolstered at the price of inflation and even fiscal solvency. While Marx did not analyze these possibilities in any detail, his overall framework has proven fruitful for understanding the contemporary role of the state in capitalist societies—in particular, how efforts to shore up demand, secure adequate accumulation, and maintain social stability have proven to be contradictory with regard to one another, creating new sources of instability.[29]

As with the theory of the business cycle, underconsumption crises have an affinity for a politics based on class struggle. Numerous (and unpredictable) actions on the part of workers, capitalists, and the state can serve to amplify or dampen the severity of the crisis. The future is regarded as open, if constrained: Collapse is not inevitable and therefore must be made to happen, in conformity with the opportunities afforded at the concrete historical moment.

Crises resulting from disproportionality: These crises stem from the unplanned nature of capitalist production. Since industries are interlinked in complex ways, with the products of one enterprise often constituting inputs into another, it is not uncommon that one industry will over- or underproduce relative to the industrial markets it confronts. Disproportionately low levels of production can result in bottlenecks, severely raising prices and adversely affecting overall industrial growth if the shortages are in goods vital to the overall economy. Conversely, an industry may produce disproportionately too many goods, resulting in growing inventories and falling prices. If the industry is central in the larger economy, such bottlenecks or over-production can reverberate widely, triggering a more generalized economic crisis, particularly if it reinforces a corresponding phase of the business cycle.

Although Marx did not analyze disproportionality crises in detail, a number of influential turn-of-the-century socialist economists[30] argued that these alone of Marx's several forms of crisis theory were inevitable. This position had an affinity for the more moderate socialist movements of the time, since it argued against the immanence of growing crisis and collapse. Rather, according to disproportionality theorists, the central economic problems of capitalism result from its anarchic, unplanned nature. Adequate state planning, which can be achieved through a peaceful transition to socialism, is therefore the remedy to be sought. (Another possibility, of course, is greater cooperation among capitalists, readily achieved through the formation of cartels, trusts, and monopolies.)

CONCLUSION: DIALECTICS AND SCIENCE

I have tried to emphasize the distinction between "tendency" and "law" as central to Marx's theory. I have argued that Marx sought to avoid the determinism associated with the natural science model, as well as the idealism that characterized his Hegelian legacy. He achieved this by conceptualizing political action as simultaneously constrained by interrelated social, economic, and political structures, while at the same time modifying these structures and thereby the conditions of future political action in a *dialectical* process.

The dialectic, as utilized by Marx in his economic analyses, entails treating socioeconomic phenomena as *necessarily* yet *contradictorily* interrelated. Such interrelationships are unstable and hence must change, although within delimited bounds and in frequently un-predictable directions. The relationship between machines and workers, conceived by Marx as a secular tendency for the organic composition of capital to rise, is a necessary yet contradictory one. It is *necessary* only under the historical "givens" of capitalist economic production: that production is for the profit of the capitalist-owner of the means of production; that capitalists compete with one another to sell their goods on the market; that workers are free to sell their labor to capitalists in exchange for a wage, rather than control over the productive process itself; and that labor-power belongs to the capitalist for the duration of the working day, rather than merely that portion of the day necessary to sustain the worker. It is *contradictory* in that it is inherently unstable: It is impossible to sustain a rising organic composition of capital indefinitely without undermining the necessary profitability on which capitalist production rests. The various requirements of profitable production, dictated by the need for economic survival under capitalist economic organization, are mutually incompatible. Each individual capitalist must sell his or her commodities at the market price or below, or suffer a decline in sales to competitors. To do so, he or she must continually seek ways to produce a larger volume of goods at lower unit costs, for that is what the competitors are doing. This requirement, in turn, engenders yet another; the need for productivity increases. Thus the individual capitalist *must* economize, and increase the output per worker through the substitution of labor-saving technologies. Over the economy as a whole, however, this has the long-run consequence of lowering profitability and hence undermining production itself. Periodic crises are thus structured into capitalist production.

While the overall tendency of the contradiction can be deduced analytically from the givens of capitalist economic production, its concrete movement cannot. That depends on historically specific circumstances. How is it that the basic conditions of the contradiction, the givens of capitalist economic production, can be modified? And how is it possible to have a "scientific theory" of economic crisis that admits of "historically specific circumstances?" These two questions are related, for they both go to the root of Marx's effort to develop a "science" of the historically concrete—one that is not predicated on universal laws and predictive statements.

We shall return to these methodological issues in the concluding chapter. First, however, it is necessary to look at those writings in which Marx most concretely applied his general theoretical framework in studying the interplay of economic and political forces: his essays on the French revolutionary periods 1848-1851 and 1870-1871.

NOTES

1. Of course this is a somewhat dubious formulation, since—as has been recognized since Darwin—such *fundamental* laws of evolution as natural selection are not species-bound.

2. The *Methodenstreit*, or debate over method in economics, occurred around the turn of the century; it pitted the Austrian School (founded by Carl Menger) against the German Historical School (Wilhelm Roscher, Karl Knies, Bruno Hildebrand, Gustav Schmoller). The former argued that economic theory was fundamentally correct in seeking to derive universally valid abstract laws after the fashion of natural science, while the latter believed that human beings often act according to noneconomic considerations (such as ethics) that are unique to each historical period, and that therefore any human science must be concrete rather than generalizing (see Burger, 1976: 140-153). A related debate concerned the *problem of meaning:* Since human beings exist in an interpretive world where meanings are socially constructed and hence highly variable, some (following Dilthey) argued that human sciences must develop procedures affording interpretive understandings rather than seeking after highly general (and therefore more superficial) regularities that result from the application of natural scientific methods (see Habermas, 1971: 140-186). Max Weber straddled these positions and addressed them directly in his methodological writings; Marx, of course, could not.

3. Among others, Lenin used this term to describe Marx's theory, which, according to Lenin, simply regarded the "superstructure" (the state in its political and legal forms, ideology, religion, philosophy, and even—according to Stalin—science and language) as a *reflection* of material conditions. See, for example, Lenin (1972).

4. Marx first announced this view in 1845 in the sixth Thesis on Feuerbach, in which he announces that "the human essence is no abstraction inherent in each single individual. In its reality it is the ensemble of the social relations" (McClellan, 1977: 157).

5. By *property* Marx primarily refers to that property that is used in subsistence production, that is, of whatever a particular society determines to be the necessities of life. Property, therefore, may include land, tools, machinery, or slaves; in any given mode of production, one type of property will predominate.

6. Other classes may exist, although these are usually treated by Marx as of secondary importance, primarily historical survivals from previous modes of production. Marx's political writings (*Eighteenth Brumaire, Class Struggles in France*) provide his most detailed treatment of a class structure in actual societies, as opposed to purely theoretical modes of production; see Chapter 6.

7. Elsewhere in his writings—notably in the *Grundrisse*—Marx identifies another mode of production, the Asiatic mode, characterized by publicly owned slaves and large-scale public works with a centralized state administration. In general, the highly rigid schema of *The German Ideology* and the *Communist Manifesto* is somewhat relaxed in the *Grundrisse*. (Near the end of his life, after following political developments in Russia, Marx even argued that Russia did not necessarily have to go through the capitalist phase in all respects before becoming communist. In a March 8, 1881, letter to the Russian socialist Vera Zasulich, Marx rejected a Russian populist's (Mikhailovski) claim to this effect as a misinterpretation of his (Marx's) writings. Marx stated that under certain conditions the Russian peasant commune "is the mainspring of Russia's social regeneration" (in McClellan, 1977: 576-577). Marx adds that the "historical inevitability" of the expropriation of the farmer "is expressly limited to the countries of Western Europe.... Thus the analysis given in *Capital* assigns no reasons for or against the vitality of the [Russian] rural community" (p. 576).

8. "This dissolution of society, as a particular class, is the proletariat.... When the proletariat proclaims the dissolution of the hitherto existing world order, it merely declares the secret of its own existence, since it is in fact the dissolution of this order" (McClellan, 1977: 73).

9. Marx had refined the distinction between labor and labor-power by the time of the

1859 contribution to *A Critique of Political Economy;* Engels posthumously revised the language of Marx's 1849 pamphlet, "Wage-Labour and Capital," accordingly (Tucker, 1972: 167).

10. That is, can readily flow from one economic activity into another.

11. The German is *Mehrwert,* or "more value."

12. There is another difference between the production of surplus under feudalism and capitalism that should be noted. Under feudalism, only the surplus is appropriated by the lord; the worker still retains substantial control over his or her tools, techniques, and the labor process in general. Under capitalism, the tools no longer are controlled by the worker, but rather the reverse; and the labor process itself is subject to the capitalist's control as the worker becomes reduced to an appendage of the assembly line. In Marx's earlier, more Hegelian language of the 1844 *Manuscripts,* under feudalism the worker becomes alienated from his or her product; under capitalism, the alienation extends to the labor process and relations with other workers as well, and is therefore complete.

13. This equation can be regarded as the value of a single commodity, or—aggregated across all commodities—the value of goods produced in a particular economic sector or throughout the economy.

14. Engels (1987), in his 1844 analysis, *The Condition of the Working Class in England,* argued that cheap housing costs would lower the cost of labor and hence wages, and that therefore workers' struggles over housing do not fundamentally alter the basis of capitalist relations or even necessarily the overall welfare of the worker.

15. This, of course, was Henry Ford's explicit strategy in mass-producing the automobile: to provide a means of transportation affordable to the mass of workers, while at the same time paying them enough to constitute a mass market for his cars.

16. Marx generally speaks of the proportion or ratio of C to V; the organic composition of capital is accordingly expressed by some writers as C/V (e.g., Mattick, 1969; Mandel, 1968). We shall follow Sweezy's (1942) usage, which defines the organic composition as the ratio of constant capital to total capital advanced. Some reformulations of Marx's theory have argued that definitions involving only the terms C and V are inadequate, since V is itself dependent in part on the rate of surplus value (exploitation) (see, e.g., Cogoy, 1973; and Wright, 1975).

17. Another purpose is control over the labor process; see Braverman (1974).

18. The algebraic derivation is as follows:

$$P = S/(C + V)$$
$$= (S/V)*V/(C + V)$$
$$= S'*[(C + V - C)/(C + V)]$$
$$= S'*[(C + V)/(C + V) - C/(C + V)]$$
$$= S'*[1 - C/(C + V)]$$
$$= S'*(1 - Q)$$

19. Sweezy (1942) notes that Marx never developed an explicit theory of crises in *Capital,* primarily because such a theory would have required a concrete analysis of particular capitalist economies, rather than the highly abstract analysis of capitalism presented in *Capital.*

20. In a sense these two are related, since the inability to realize the value of goods through sale is destabilizing only insofar as it depresses the capitalist's profits. The distinction is useful, however, in that profitability crises impede the production of goods, while realization crises impede the sale of goods already produced. To the extent that the latter reduce profitability, of course, future production will be curtailed as well.

21. In Marx's terminology, wages are kept at the value of the commodity "labor," with value defined in terms of the cost of production of the commodity (in this case, subsistence requirements). When any commodity is scarce—including labor—its price will temporarily rise above its value, until the higher price results in greater production, oversupply, and hence the restoration of the equilibrium price that again reflects value.

22. In terms of equation 4, S is reinvested in V, to the detriment of P and possibly C; this impedes both accumulation and profitability.

23. The loss in value of idle machinery may also contribute to the restoration of profit. In equation 4, both terms in the denominator (C and V) may decrease during a period of economic decline; the empirical question is whether the numerator (S) declines by a lesser amount.

24. See also 1973 (pp. 338-340) for a crude mathematical argument. See Wright (1975: 37, footnote 7) and Yaffe (1973: 202) for an attempt at a mathematical demonstration that, "as the organic composition of capital rises, the rate of profit becomes progressively less sensitive to changes in the rate of exploitation (i.e., surplus value)" (Wright, 1975: 16).

25. In Volume 3, Part III of *Capital* (pp. 232-240), Marx discusses six counteracting influences on the tendency of the rate of profit to fall: increasing the intensity of exploitation, depression of wages below the value of labor power, cheapening the elements of constant capital, relative overpopulation, foreign trade, and the increase of stock capital.

26. In terms of equation 4, the individual capitalist, driven to maximize profits in order to remain competitive, must seek to maximize S, reinvesting in C; V thus declines relative to the other terms in the equation, the organic composition (equation 3) rises, and aggregate demand falls (represented by V, aggregated across the economy).

27. In *Wage-Labour and Capital* (lectures given by Marx in 1847), Marx argued that workers become impoverished relative to capitalists, even during periods of economic growth, since the latters' standard of living rises significantly more than that of the former, widening the gulf between the two. While this would not necessarily have an adverse economic impact in terms of aggregate demand, it can still lead to worker discontent and hence revolutionary activity: "Our desires and pleasures spring from society; we measure them, therefore, by society and not by the objects that serve for their satisfaction. Because they are of a social nature, they are of a relative nature" (in McClellan, 1977: 259).

28. See, e.g., Sweezy (1942: Chapter 6) for a related discussion.

29. O'Connor's (1973) notion of the "fiscal crisis of the state" has proven extremely fruitful in this regard.

30. Notably, the Russian economist Tugan-Baronowsky, and the German economist Hilferding.

6

Economic Structures and Political Action

Marx's most sustained theoretical analysis of capitalism—contained in the fully completed first volume of *Capital*—is primarily an exercise in economic modeling. While Marx draws heavily on British economic statistics to sustain his argument, overall *Capital* moves at a high level of generality, a model of a "pure" capitalist mode of production rather than an empirical study of any particular economy or society. Marx's analysis is unique in that it reveals the structured instabilities that provide the opportunities for social change. But the details of such change cannot be inferred from the model itself; they depend, as we saw at the end of the last chapter, on concrete circumstances. These cannot be studied abstractly—only historically.

In other words, Marx's theoretical categories must be concretely grounded in actual societies and social movements if they are to provide us with an understanding of how social change actually occurs. Fortunately, Marx offers us just such an analysis in his journalistic studies of the French workers' uprisings during the periods 1848-1851 and 1870-1871. In this chapter we review those writings that provide some insight into Marx's empirical treatment of the dialectic between structure and action. We shall begin with a discussion of Marx's treatment of the state, both as an instrument of domination and as a partly autonomous arena for change. We will then turn to a discussion of politics and action, focusing on two central issues: the principal agents of social change, and the question of revolutionary violence.

Finally, we will discuss Marx's vision of the future, in terms of both social and political organization.

The Role of the State:
Instrumentalism vs. Relative Autonomy

Marx often writes as if the state in capitalist society were simply an instrument through which the ruling class exerts its power over society as a whole. This is asserted in the *Communist Manifesto,* in which Marx explicitly contends that "political power, properly so called, is merely the organized power of one class for oppressing another" (in McClellan, 1977: 238). Marx holds this to be true of all class societies, including the liberal democratic state associated with the emergent capitalism of his time:

> Each step in the development of the bourgeoisie was accompanied by a corresponding political advance of that class. . . . The bourgeoisie has at last, since the establishment of Modern Industry and of the world-market, conquered for itself, in the modern representative State, exclusive political sway. *The executive of the modern state is but a committee for managing the affairs of the whole bourgeoisie.* [*Communist Manifesto;* in McClellan, 1977: 223; emphasis added]

According to this view, the modern universalistic state is but a smokescreen, masking the narrow concerns of the ruling class as the common interest. Electoral politics is but a sham, existing solely for the purpose "of deciding once in three or six years which member of the ruling class [is] to misrepresent the people in Parliament" ("The Civil War in France"; in McClellan, 1977: 543). Bourgeois ideology falsely claims the liberal state to be an arena where a plurality of interests contend, with democratic processes secured through Constitutional safeguards and a generalized belief in the legitimacy of the rule of law. Such an ideology is promulgated by the ruling class, which by virtue of its economic and political power is capable of effectively propagandizing through the educational system and its control over the mass media.

This fairly simple *instrumental model* served a useful didactic purpose that Marx wielded effectively in the *Manifesto* and other programmatic writings. As we shall see, however, in his more substantive analyses he neither adhered to a simple ruling-class model, nor viewed the state in such simple instrumental terms. Wealthy and powerful capitalists will of course seek to bend the state to their own interests, but their success will depend on the concrete historical circumstances, which cannot be inferred from the model itself. In other words, the instrumental model must be regarded as a pure type, revealing a *political tendency* embedded within the dynamics of capitalist economic production. This, in turn, is viewed as the likely outcome of the *economic tendencies* toward monopolization and centralization of economic power, and the bifurcation of society into two great warring classes. The pure type provides a framework for analyzing the emergent reality, against which it must always be judged.

When Marx engages in such a concrete analysis, the resulting picture is much more complex than the simple instrumental model would suggest. For example, while he regards the liberal democratic state as the form most appropriate to capitalism, he also recognizes that the same economic system can give rise to different political systems, and that sometimes politics can dominate economics rather than the reverse (McClellan, 1975: 62-64). As we shall see below, when conflicting classes (or parts of classes) are of nearly equal strength—as they were in France during the period surrounding the Second Empire under Napoleon III—the state can enjoy a fair degree of *relative autonomy* from purely economic interests.[1]

Voting is of particular interest to Marx, since universal suffrage is a key mechanism by which the state is legitimated in capitalist society. Elections, as Marx seeks to demonstrate, are a double-edged sword. On the one hand, under the economic and political conditions that existed in nineteenth-century England, suffrage served to promote socialist ends:

> Universal Suffrage is the equivalent of political power in England, where the proletariat forms the large majority of the population, where, in a long, though underground civil war, it has gained a clear consciousness of itself as a class, and where even the rural districts know no longer any peasants, but only landlords, industrial capitalists (farmers), and hired labourers. The carrying of Universal Suffrage in England would, therefore, be a far more socialistic measure than anything which has been honoured with that name on the Continent. ["The Chartists" [1852]; reproduced in Avineri, 1968: 214][2]

On the other hand, as Marx shows in some detail in his study of the Second French Republic (1848-1852), suffrage can have much more complex and occasionally perverse consequences; it was obviously never intended by the French bourgeoisie to promote communism. They fostered it under the false belief that voting would buttress their position; yet it instead undermined their interests by forcing "the political rule of the bourgeoisie into democratic conditions, which at every moment help the hostile classes to victory and jeopardize the very foundations of bourgeois society" ("The Class Struggles in France"; in McClellan, 1977: 292). In this instance, universal suffrage meant the election of Napoleon III, largely due to the strong support of the French peasantry. Napoleon's election, in turn, paved the way for his December 1851 overthrow of the Republic.

In general, then, while the right to vote under capitalism can never hope truly to empower the working class, it can under certain circumstances advance their interests, and it does at least provide for a small check on what otherwise might be the unbridled power of the economic elites. On the other hand, Marx holds that suffrage can also have adverse consequences for workers, such as when it makes conservative groups such as the French peasantry a deciding force in politics (Avineri, 1968: 212-214).[3] The meaning of the vote, like everything else for Marx, depends on the concrete circumstances under which it is exercised.

Politics and Action

Marx's analysis of British capitalism provides a framework for understanding the economic forces at work in the most advanced capitalist society of his time. Yet *Capital* offers only a framework; economic forces are realized in practice only within institutions created and sustained by human actors. It is through our social practices that we both reproduce and modify that institutional environment. Marx is largely concerned with a particular set of social practices—those oriented toward shaping economic and political institutions. He argues that to a large extent such practices are organized along class lines, rather than reflecting the independent decisions of individual political actors. Only individuals acting in concert—and in keeping with forces already present in society—can hope to have any measure of success in shaping history to their conscious ends.

Class and Class Practices

In the *Communist Manifesto,* Marx boldly asserts that "society as a whole is more and more splitting up into two great hostile camps, into two great classes directly facing each other: Bourgeoisie and Proletariat" (in McClellan, 1977: 222). He then briefly charts the evolution of this tendency, beginning with the decline of feudalism and culminating with the absorption of other classes into one or the other of these two great classes:

> Of all the classes that stand face to face with the bourgeoisie today, the
> proletariat alone is the really revolutionary class. The other classes decay

and finally disappear in the face of Modern Industry; the proletariat is its special and essential product. [in McClellan, 1977: 229]

This broad description follows from Marx's economic analysis, which—although fully fleshed out some 20 years after the above passage was written in 1848—nonetheless existed in schematic form at the time of the *Manifesto*.[4] As we saw in Chapter 5, Marx sought to demonstrate that capitalist economic production entailed strong tendencies toward mechanization and automation, monopoly ownership and control over key industries, the deskilling and pauperization of labor, and a polarized class society. As with all such general tendencies, the actual working-out of these forces was seen as dependent on particular circumstances. Marx's journalistic studies of mid-nineteenth-century France and Germany offer an excellent insight into how Marx's general theoretical framework can be utilized to analyze the joint impact of political practices and economic conditions, resulting in a much more complex class analysis than is suggested in the passages from the *Manifesto* cited above.[5]

The period 1848-1851 was marked by workers' protests and revolutionary ferment throughout the European continent. In France, the July Revolution of 1830 had overthrown the monarchy and established the position of Constitutional Monarch with Louis Philippe, the Duke of Orleans, on the throne. Louis Philippe was able to retain his hold on government only through vigorous repression of the radical organizations that flourished among the French proletariat and intelligentsia, but the economic depression of 1846-1847 finally destroyed his power base and, in February 1848, forced his abdication in the face of a threatened armed workers' uprising. Riding this crest of worker militancy, the socialist Louis Blanc sought to declare a workers' state, only to be beaten back in the bourgeois-controlled Constituent Assembly, which instead declared the Second Republic. In December 1848 Louis Napoleon Bonaparte—"the nephew of his uncle," as Marx ("The Class Struggles in France"; in McClellan, 1977: 293) derisively called him—was elected president of the Second Republic, which he dissolved three years later, declaring himself emperor.[6]

French industrial development proceeded rapidly under the Bonapartist (Second) Empire. But Napoleon's attempt to restore the borders of the First Empire (lost in 1814) led to France's defeat in the Franco-Prussian War of 1870. With Paris encircled by Prussian troops, the French National Assembly created the Third Republic, its leadership centered in neighboring Versailles. The Parisian workers rejected the Third Republic. Mindful of their fate under the bourgeois-dominated Second Republic 20 years earlier, they renounced it as a front for the interests of the bourgeoisie. Paris instead rose up in arms and declared its own socialist republic. For several months (March to May 1871) the Paris Commune withstood the threat of Prussian invasion, offering a socialist alternative to Versailles. The Third Republic was eventually forced to appeal for Prussian assistance in retaking Paris.

Marx identified a number of classes and "class factions" as significant in shaping French politics during the first revolutionary period 1848-1850. The bourgeoisie was divided into two powerful and antagonistic factions: the finance aristocracy—consisting of the "bankers, stock exchange kings, railway kings, owners of coal and iron mines and forests, a part of the landed proprietors associated with them" ("The Class Struggles in France"; in McClellan, 1977: 286)—and the industrial bourgeoisie. The former alone ruled under Louis Philippe, with the latter in the position of Parliamentary minority. The power of the financiers was viewed by Marx as antithetical to the development of capitalism, since they sought "to get rich not by production, but by pocketing the already available wealth of others" (in McClellan, 1977: 288) in deriving their wealth from the tax-financed state debt:

> The July monarchy was nothing other than a joint-stock company for the exploitation of France's national wealth, the dividends of which were divided among ministers, Chambers, 240,000 voters, and their adherents. Louis Philippe was the director of this company. [in McClellan, 1977: 288]

Other classes regarded by Marx as significant during this period included the peasantry, the petty bourgeoisie (primarily small shop-keepers), and, of course, the proletariat, whom Marx saw as the sole standard-bearer of radical change. The army and the national guard also played key roles. To each class corresponds a political group or party:

> And yet the state power is not suspended in mid air. Bonaparte represents a class, and the most numerous class of French society at that, the small-holding peasants.

> Just as the Bourbons were the dynasty of landed property and just as the Orleans were the dynasty of money, so the Bonapartes are the dynasty of the peasants, that is, the mass of the French people. [*Eighteenth Brumaire;* in McClellan, 1977: 317]

By 1848 the industrial bourgeoisie had stepped up its opposition to the financial aristocracy, secure in its belief that the workers—decisively defeated in the earlier uprisings—were no longer a threat. At the same time economic conditions were increasingly adverse: The "potato blight and the crop failures of 1845 and 1846 increased the general ferment among the people, while the dearth of 1847 called forth bloody conflicts in France as well as the rest of the Continent" ("The Class Struggles in France"; in McClellan, 1977: 289). These conditions were exacerbated by the English commercial and industrial crises of 1845-1847, which closed English markets to French manufacturers and traders, forcing the latter to set up their own establishments—"the competition of which ruined the small epiciers [grocers] and boutiquiers [shopkeepers] en masse" (in McClellan, 1977: 290).

This constellation of political interests and economic conditions culminated in workers' uprisings and street fighting, eventually forcing the monarchy to abdicate to a provisional government. Although the uprisings were successful in this regard, they did not initially succeed in forcing the provisional government to restore a Republican form of government. This occurred only when the leaders threatened to storm the seat of government with an army of a quarter million workers. Marx comments that although the workers regarded the February Republic as a victory, their hopes for a social revolution were a "singular contradiction to everything that with the material available, with the degree of education attained by the masses, under the circumstances and relations, could immediately be realized in practice" (*Eighteenth Brumaire;* in Zeitlin, 1967: 137). For, as Marx always emphasized, society "has in truth first to create for itself the revolutionary point of departure, the situation, the relations, the conditions under which alone modern revolution becomes serious" (*Eighteenth Brumaire;* in McClellan, 1977: 302).

The material conditions were not ripe for social revolution. "Every fairly competent observor, even if he had not followed the course of French development step by step, must have had a presentiment that an unheard-of fiasco was in store for the revolution" (*Eighteenth Brumaire;* in McClellan, 1977: 303). In the French revolts of 1830 and 1848, the radical support of the proletariat had been the key to success—yet the bourgeoisie turned on its former ally as soon as the revolution was secured. No successful bourgeois revolution (in Marx's view) was possible without proletarian support (Zeitlin, 1967: 148-149). In 1848, for example, in order to wrest power from the financial aristocracy while curbing the proletariat's demands, the industrialists needed to divide workers from the French peasantry. This was accomplished partly through the passage of a tax that fell heavily on the peasants, who then blamed the workers, seen as its chief beneficiaries. The bourgeoisie finally provoked the proletariat to the June insurrection, in which—

pitted against all other classes and factions—they were brutally crushed. While this act secured the Second Republic for the bourgeoisie, it also removed the only obstacle to Louis Napoleon's peasant-based coup in 1851—the proletariat.

Napoleon's role was of special interest to Marx, who regarded his power as deriving from the fact that he symbolized all things to all people. "Thus it happened . . . that the most simple-minded man in France acquired the most multifarious significance. Just because he was nothing, he could signify everything save himself." ("The Class Struggles in France"; in McClellan, 1977: 294). To the peasants he was the "uncle"; they elected him president in December 1848 correctly believing he would eventually overthrow the Republic and restore the greatness of the First Empire.

> The other classes helped to complete the election victory of the peasants. To the proletariat, the election of Napoleon meant the deposition of Cavaignac [a general who helped put down the June 1848 insurrection], the overthrow of the Constitutent Assembly, the dismissal of bourgeois republicanism, the cassation of the June victory. To the petty bourgeoisie, Naopleon meant the rule of the debtor over the creditor. For the majority of the big bourgeoisie, the election of Napoleon meant an open breach with the faction of which it had to make use, for a moment, against the revolution, but which became intolerable to it as soon as this faction sought to consolidate the position of the moment into a constitutional position. ["The Class Struggles in France"; in McClellan, 1977: 294]

Marx's discussion of the French peasantry, characterized as "the class that represents barbarism within civilization" ("The Class Struggles in France"; in McClellan, 1977: 293), reveals the importance of consciousness in Marx's conceptualization of social class:

> The small-holding peasants form a vast mass, the members of which live in similar conditions but without entering into manifold relations with one another. Their mode of production isolates them from one another instead of bringing them into mutual intercourse. The isolation is increased by France's bad means of communication and by the poverty of the peasants. . . . In this way, the great mass of the French nation is formed by the simple addition of homologous multitudes, much as potatoes in a sack form a sack of potatoes. . . . In so far as there is a merely local interconnection among these small-holding peasants, and the identity of their interests begets no community, no national bond, and no political organization among them, they do not form a class. [*Eighteenth Brumaire;* in McClellan, 1977: 317-318]

Whatever its objective position vis-à-vis the mode of production, a group of people does not function as a class unless they possess a self-conscious awareness of their social location and political role. That is why the proletariat is seen as the first social class in history to have the potential consciously to transform society. The proletariat, thrust together in factories and workhouses, is capable of correctly understanding the structural sources of their oppression:

> The advance of industry, whose involuntary promoter is the bourgeoisie, replaces the isolation of the labourers, due to competition, by their revolutionary combination, due to association. [*Communist Manifesto;* in McClellan, 1977: 231]

That understanding is, of course, seen as being provided by the Communist Party, which is

> on the one hand, practically, the most advanced and resolute section of the working-class parties of every country, that section which pushes forward all others; on the other hand, theoretically, they have over the mass of the proletariat the advantage of clearly understanding the line of march, the conditions, and the ultimate general results of the proletarian movement. [*Communist Manifesto;* in McClellan, 1977: 231]

Revolution and Counter-Revolution similarly explains the failure of revolution in Germany in terms of the combined forces of economics, social structure, and history. According to Marx's and Engels's analysis, the old German feudal nobility remained powerful, while the nascent German bourgeoisie was economically and politically underdeveloped. This was primarily attributed to Germany's geographical distance from the principal Atlantic world trade routes, as well as the nearly continuous warfare that had been waged on German soil from the sixteenth century onward. Even as its economic strength grew, however, the bourgeoisie was politically weakened by the atomistic German constitutional structure, which divided the nation into 36 semi-autonomous principalities united by a ponderous bureaucracy. The petty bourgeoisie was much more numerous in Germany than elsewhere on the Continent, largely because the industrial bourgeoisie was underdeveloped; and the latter was politically dependent on the monarchy and aristocracy. The most numerous class—the German farmers—were categorized by Marx into wealthy land barons, small freeholders, feudal tenants, and agricultural workers. Given this situation, the German proletariat was extremely weak, possessing very poorly developed class consciousness. With the bourgeoisie both internally divided and politically retrograde, the German revolutionary uprisings of 1848 stood no chance of success. Under this complex of socioeconomic forces not even a successful bourgeois revolution was possible, and in 1849 a German nation was proclaimed with the Prussian king at its head.

Even in these brief summaries it is clear that Marx does not attempt to reduce politics to economics. As Engels (letter to Conrad Schmidt; quoted in Zeitlin, 1967: 140) later commented,

> If therefore [anyone] supposes that we deny any and every reaction, of the political, etc. reflexes of the economic movement upon the movement itself, he is simply tilting at windmills. He has only to look at Marx's *18th Brumaire,* which deals almost exclusively with the particular part played by political struggles and events, of course within their general dependence upon economic conditions.[7]

Marx's two-class model was not seen in Paris, much less elsewhere in France. This virtually assured the failure of the workers' revolution, which could not succeed until, according to Marx, "it had aroused the masses of the nation, peasants and petty bourgeoisie" (in Zeitlin, 1967: 132).

Although economic interests are related to political groupings, the relationship is seldom straightforward: While political actors may eventually be expected to pursue their economic self-interests, in the short run there is considerable room for variation. Marx's theory tells us what to expect in the broadest sense, providing an ideal type against which to judge the movement of concrete historical events.

Revolutionary Violence and Class Consciousness

In Marx's view, how one brings about social change is an inseparable component of the changes that are achieved. The proletariat is itself transformed by the process transforming society. As Avineri (1968: 143) puts it,

> Objectively, it is the organization of the conditions leading towards ultimate human emancipation. Subjectively it is the self-change the proletariat achieves by its self-discovery through organization. . . . Organization and association . . . change the worker, his way of life, his consciousness of himself and his society.

This, of course, is the notion of praxis, and it has a number of implications for revolutionary strategy. First, it makes theoretical understanding both the prerequisite for, and outcome of, successful social change. An adequate revolutionary consciousness on the part of the workers must comprehend the possibilities inherent in the present moment, yet be flexible enough to alter its understanding in light of the ongoing revolutionary experience.

Second, the notion of praxis makes it clear that while material conditions may create the opportunity for effective revolutionary action, by themselves they do not ensure success: The level of workers' consciousness must be sufficient as well. Class consciousness must be raised through the educational activities of the International, as well as trade union activities and economic struggles in general.

Finally, the notion of praxis implies that clandestine revolutionary activities, while perhaps necessary under certain repressive conditions, are less desirable than open class struggle. Sectarian movements are both an indicator that the time for revolutionary change is not ripe, and are themselves likely to be corrupting experiences. Zeitlin (1967: 59-60) offers the following succinct summary of Marx's position:

> Marx condemned conspiratorial revolutionaries who wished to capture power and introduce socialism before the economic base of society had developed to the point at which the working class as a whole is ready to participate in the revolution. . . . He saw his role as raising the revolutionary consciousness of workers and preparing for the revolution that would occur when conditions were ripe.

Marx condemns socialist sectarianism in no uncertain terms:

> The development of socialist sectarianism and that of the real working-class movement always stand in reverse ratio to each other. Sects are justified (historically) so long as the working class is not yet ripe for an independent historical movement. As soon as it has attained this maturity all sects are essentially reactionary . . . out of the separate economic movements of the workers there grows up everywhere a political movement, that is to say a movement of the class, with the object of enforcing its interests in a general form, in a form possessing general, socially coercive force. While these movements presuppose a certain degree of previous organisation, they are in turn equally a means of developing this organization. [letter to Friedrich Bolte, Secretary of the American Federal Council of the International, November 23, 1871; reproduced in McClellan, 1977: 587-589]

As Avineri (1968: 238) concludes, "a revolutionary movement based on terror, intimidation and blackmail will ultimately produce a society based on these methods as well." If one attempts to force revolutionary change through sectarian organizations before the time is ripe, Jacobinism—the terror of the guillotine—is the likely consequence. Marx opposed the use of terror, repeatedly condemned unnecessary conspiracies, and far preferred overt to covert action. In his 1874-1875 criticism of Bakunin's *Statism and Anarchy,* for example, Marx derisively commented:

> What a wonderful example of barracks-communism! Everything is here: common pots and dormitories, control commissioners and comptoirs, the regulation of education, production, and consumption—in one word, of all social activity; and at the top, our Committee, anonymous and unknown, as supreme direction. [reproduced in Avineri, 1968: 238]

Fifteen years earlier, in *Herr Vogt* (1860), Marx pointed out that despite being forced underground by repression, the League of Communists had always attempted to raise consciousness through libraries, schooling, and lectures, rather than get embroiled in plots and coups (Avineri, 1968: 146). In a similar vein, Friedrich Lessner—who was involved in the 1847 reorganization of the League of the Just into the League of Communists—reports that Marx eliminated the conspiratorial element from the latter (Avineri, 1968: 147), a conclusion that is supported by Nicolaievsky and Menchen-Helfen (1936). Summarizing Marx's position on the importance of democracy in waging revolutionary struggle, Avineri (1968: 70) concludes that

> on the whole, Marx was in favor of open, democratic organization, with decisions taken by majority vote at national conferences . . . he did insist that [the] party should have a completely democratic internal organization; that it should be the independent creation of the workers themselves; that it should be distinguished by a theoretical understanding of working-class goals.

This is not to imply that Marx renounced the use of force in making revolution. As with other aspects of his theory of social change, Marx is reluctant to establish general principles, arguing instead that the concrete circumstances will dictate the appropriate methods to be used. Under certain circumstances—notably, the presence of democratic institutions, universal suffrage, and a highly developed industrial base—violence is unnecessary for the proletariat to attain power: "We do not deny that there are countries like England and America and if I am familiar with your institutions, Holland, where labour may attain its goal by peaceful means" (from Marx's September 18, 1872, speech at the

Hague Congress of the International; reproduced in Avineri, 1968: 216). On the other hand, militant action may be warranted when conditions are suboptimal. Marx felt this was true of the European Continent, but worried that the need for more violent methods implied that neither the external conditions nor workers' consciousness were ready for revolution.[8] By the founding of the First International in 1864, Marx had come to believe that workers could make real gains under capitalism, acknowledging, for example, the emergence of a labor aristocracy in England (McClellan, 1975: 66-67). In fact, toward the end of his life Marx feared that the very real achievements gained by English workers had muted their revolutionary fervor:

> [The] party considers an English revolution not *necessary*, but— according to historic precedents—*possible*. If the unavoidable evolution turns into a revolution, it would not only be the fault of the ruling classes, but also of the working class . . . if [their pressure] has more and more weakened, it is only because the English working class know not how to wield their power and use their liberties, both of which they possess legally. [Marx to Henry M. Hyndman, founder of the Social Democratic Federation, December 8, 1880; reproduced in McClellan, 1977: 594]

The Future Society

Although Marx frequently wrote as if communism were inevitable, he regarded the future as a potential to be realized through political action. The dialectics of structure and action would shape the future, which could never be predicted on the basis of theory alone. This unwillingness to engage in utopian speculation probably accounts for Marx's reluctance to devote much attention to describing life and politics in the future society. Communism would grow out of tendencies already present in capitalist society, with its final character defined through the actual process of creating a social revolution. Marx was far more interested in analyzing current events than predicting future ones.

I have commented (Chapter 5) that Marx was remarkably accurate in anticipating the long-term development of capitalism. He foresaw its worldwide character, its revolutionizing technology that would eventually result in the complete automation of industry, and its tendencies toward monopoly ownership and centralization of control. When Marx felt impelled by current events to make more short-term predictions, however, he was often proven incorrect—as when, in the wake of the failed 1848 revolutions, he wrote in 1850 that "a new revolution is possible only in the wake of a new crisis. It is, however, just as certain as this crisis" (quoted in Zeitlin, 1967: 142). The anticipated economic crisis never came, however.[9]

Having offered these caveats, let me add yet another: It is beside the point to observe that Marx's predictions concerning communist society, including its minimalist form of governance, have never been realized in practice. Marx was writing at the beginning of capitalism, in an essentially rural world existing at a comparatively (relative to today) low level of both population and technological development. There is no way he could have drafted a blueprint for the state or society of the latter twentieth century. Nor, as I have indicated, would he have sought to do so, since it would have violated his most basic assumptions concerning the relationship between theory and practice.

Communism and Human Nature

As we saw in Chapter 4, Marx initially viewed people as by nature capable of realizing fulfillment through cooperative, conscious endeavor. While in his later works he often treated human nature as reflecting social conditions and therefore malleable, he never abandoned the position that human potential is severely stunted in class society.

To the extent that he writes about it at all, communism—to use Zeitlin's (1967: 60) entirely appropriate phrase—is treated as "paradise on earth." Marx, perhaps reflecting his early immersion in the Greek classics, believed that the individual and society enjoy a fundamentally harmonious relationship; unlike Plato, however, he also believed that such a harmony could be achieved only when society is fundamentally reorganized along communal lines. As Zeitlin (1967: 62) put it,

> Greed, egoism and envy are not engrained forever in the character of human beings. They would disappear in a society in which private property and private means of production were replaced with communal property and socially organized means of production.

In terms of both social organization and political structure, Marx tends to see two stages to the development of the future society. As he writes in his 1875 *Critique of the [German socialist] Gotha Program,*

> Between capitalist and communist society lies the period of the revolutionary transformation of the one into the other. Corresponding to this is also a political transition period in which the state can be nothing but the revolutionary dictatorship of the proletariat.
>
> What we have to deal with here is a communist society, not as it has developed on its own foundations, but, on the contrary, just as it emerges

from capitalist society; which is thus in every respect, economically, morally, and intellectually, still stamped with the birthmarks of the old society from whose womb it emerges. [in McClellan, 1977: 565, 568]

The first, transitional stage involves the consolidation of the revolution in the face of opposition (if not open counterrevolutionary activity) on the part of the deposed capitalist class and its international allies. During this stage the economy has to be fundamentally reorganized, new governmental institutions have to be created, and the traumatic effects of the revolution have to be surmounted. Economic scarcity may also be a problem, depending on the prior development of the productive forces, the international setting, and, of course, the destruction wrought by the revolution.

During this first stage private ownership of the means of production is abolished, and they become instead the common property of all the productive members of society. The economy is administered by a greatly reduced state apparatus (see next section). Workers are remunerated according to their contribution to the economy, crudely indexed by the length of time they labor. Marx concedes that this form of equality is nothing more than the realization of "bourgeois right . . . an unequal right for unequal labour . . . [since] it tacitly recognizes unequal individual endowment and productive capacity as natural privileges" (Gotha; in McClellan, 1977: 568-569). But, with characteristic realism, Marx goes on to assert that one can never expect more than the material conditions permit:

> But these defects are inevitable in the first phase of communist society as it is when it has just emerged after prolonged birth pangs from capitalist society. Right can never be higher than the economic structure of society and its cultural development conditioned thereby. [Gotha; in McClellan, 1977: 569]

During the second and final stage, true communist society is realized. Competitive social relations cease, the division of labor is abolished, full creative potential is realized, and alienation disappears as industrial discipline is reduced.[10] Marx's well-known description of this utopia is contained in The German Ideology, written 30 years earlier:

> For as soon as the distribution of labour comes into being, each man has a particular, exclusive sphere of activity, which is forced upon him and from which he cannot escape. He is a hunter, a fisherman, a shepherd, or a critical critic, and must remain so if he does not want to lose his means of livelihood; while in communist society, where nobody has one exclusive

sphere of activity but each can become accomplished in any branch he wishes, society regulates the general production and thus makes it possible for me to do one thing today and another tomorrow, to hunt in the morning, to fish in the afternoon, rear cattle in the evening, criticize after dinner, just as I have a mind, without ever becoming hunter, fisherman, shepherd or critic. [in McClellan, 1977: 169]

While Marx in his earlier writings argued that labor will be a positive experience in communist society—performed, as it is, for the common good in a nonexploitive and cooperative environment—he had apparently concluded by the time *Capital* was completed that true human freedom is achieved only after the working day ends:[11]

In fact, the realm of freedom actually begins only where labour which is determined by necessity and mundane considerations ceases; thus in the very nature of things it lies beyond the sphere of actual material production. . . . Beyond it begins the development of human energy which is an end in itself, the true realm of freedom, which, however, can blossom forth only with this realm of necessity as its basis. *The shortening of the working day is its basic prerequisite.* [*Capital,* Volume 3: 830; emphasis added]

For this utopia to be realized, several conditions must be met. Technology must be sufficiently developed to permit a significant reduction in the labor-time required to produce the desired level of consumption—what Marx terms the "socially necessary labour time" (see Chapter 5). The "realm of freedom" achieved under communism is definitely dependent on relative material abundance, which results from the strong development of technology under capitalism—along with the abolition of wasteful competition, the substitution of efficient economic planning, and the abolition of surplus labor-time (beyond that needed for capital accumulation). It also assumes that growth in the productive forces outstrip the growth in human wants:

With his development this realm of physical necessity expands as a result of his wants; but, at the same time, the forces of production which satisfy these wants also increases. Freedom in this field can only consist in socialised man, the associated producers, rationally regulating their interchange with Nature, bringing it under their common control, instead of being ruled by it as by the blind forces of Nature; and achieving this with the least expenditure of energy and under conditions most favourable to, and worthy of, their human nature. [*Capital,* Volume 3: 830]

While it is presumably an open question whether such technological and organizational changes will permit output to grow faster than human wants,[12] Marx clearly assumes this to be the case. He (1973: 705-706) makes his argument most forcefully in the 1857-1858 *Grundrisse:*

> But to the degree that large industry develops, the creation of real wealth comes to depend less on labour time and on the amount of labour employed than on the power of the agencies set in motion during labour time, whose "powerful effectiveness" is itself in turn out of all proportion to the direct labour time spent on their production, but depends rather on the general state of science and on the progress of technology, or the application of this science to production. . . . The free development of individualities, and hence not the reduction of necessary labour time so as to posit surplus labour, but rather the general reduction of the necessary labour of society to a minimum, which then corresponds to the artistic, scientific, etc. development of the individuals in the time set free, and with the means created, for all of them.

In the same passage from the *Grundrisse,* Marx brilliantly anticipates the manner in which automation will eventually reduce the need for human labor in production, as "the human being comes to relate more as watchman and regulator to the production process itself" (1973: 705). Improved technology, rational economic organization, and a highly motivated work force will thus raise the level of output to the point where workers need no longer be rewarded according to their labor-time. Instead, in Marx's celebrated phrase,

> only then can the narrow horizon of bourgeois right be crossed in its entirety and society inscribe on its banners: *from each according to his ability, to each according to his needs!* [*Critique of the Gotha Program;* in McClellan, 1977: 569; emphasis added]

The State in Communist Society

Given Marx's view of the state as primarily an instrument of class domination, it is not surprising that he believes it will become largely superfluous in classless communist society. Marx advocates the abolition of state power only when social conditions render it anachronistic—after it has outlived its usefulness.[13] This will occur only during the second stage of communism as described above.

In the *Communist Manifesto,* Marx lays out the details of proletarian rule during the first, transitional stage:

> The proletariat will use its political supremacy to wrest, by degrees, all capital from the bourgeoisie, to centralise all instruments of production in the hands of the State, i.e., of the producers organized as the ruling class; and to increase the total of productive forces as rapidly as possible. . . . Of

course, in the beginning this cannot be effected except by means of despotic inroads on the rights of property, and on the conditions of bourgeois production. [in McClellan, 1977: 237]

Such "despotic inroads" can be achieved only by a strong central state run by the working class—a "dictatorship of the proletariat."[14] In the *Communist Manifesto,* Marx called for a 10-point program that assumed the existing state machinery could be seized by the workers and used for their own ends. The most radical features of this program included the abolition of landed property, the creation of a state bank with a monopoly on credit, the establishment of a state monopoly on communication and transport, and the extension of state ownership of the means of production.[15] Full social ownership of the economy would occur gradually, rather than through forced expropriation of private industry. These were not especially radical proposals, even at the time; all were nascent within capitalism, representing the fruition of existing tendencies (Avineri, 1968: 207).

In the nearly quarter century between the completion of the *Communist Manifesto* and the 1871 Paris Commune—after the abortive 1848 uprisings and the violent suppression of the Commune by the Versailles government—Marx was forced to conclude that "the working class cannot simply lay hold of the ready-made state machinery, and wield it for its own purposes" ("The Civil War in France"; in McClellan, 1977: 539). In his April 12, 1871, letter to Ludwig Kugelman, Marx added that

the next attempt of the French Revolution will be no longer, as before, to transfer the bureaucratic-military machinery from one hand to another, but to smash it; and this is the preliminary condition for every real people's revolution on the Continent. [in McClellan, 1977: 592][16]

The model for the transitional "dictatorship of the proletariat" became the Paris Commune itself.[17] Marx did not initially support the Commune, since he believed that under existing conditions the insurrection would be destroyed by factional strife and external warfare (Avineri, 1968: 245). Although expunged from the final version, earlier drafts of "The Civil War in France" indicate that Marx viewed the Commune as more petty bourgeois than working class (Avineri, 1968: 247). But he strongly supported the democratic form of governance adopted by the Commune, which he approvingly described in "The Civil War in France" in the following terms:

The Commune was formed of the municipal councillors, chosen by universal suffrage in the various wards of the town, responsible and revocable at short terms. The majority of its members were naturally working men, or acknowledged representatives of the working class. The Commune was to be a working, not Parliamentary, body, executive and legislative at the same time. Instead of continuing to be an agent of the Central Government, the police was at once stripped of its political attributes, and turned into the responsible and at all times revocable agent of the Commune. So were the officials of all other branches of the Administration. From the members of the Commune downwards, the public service had to be done at workmen's wages. The vested interests and the representation allowances of the high dignitaries of State disappeared along with the high dignitaries themselves. Public functions ceased to be the private property of the tools of the Central Government. . . . The priests were sent back to the recesses of private life. . . . The whole of the educational institutions were opened to the people gratuitously, and at the same time cleared of all interference of Church and State. . . . Like the rest of public servants, magistrates and judges were to be elective, responsible, and revocable. [in McClellan, 1977: 541-542]

Marx especially liked the Commune's direct election (and dismissal) of all public servants, which he believed would provide for much greater accountability than the ordinary legislative model. The people, Marx felt, should be able to hire and fire their representatives, much as any business is able to do with its workers. Universal suffrage under these circumstances meant far more than mere parliamentarism: It reflected a high degree of mass political involvement, a prerequisite for a state power that will eventually abolish itself (Avineri, 1968: 212).

Had it survived, the Commune was to have been the model for a communist France. Its proposed national government—which Marx also describes approvingly—thus serves as a general description of the role of the state in a fully developed communist society:

In a rough sketch of national organization which the Commune had no time to develop, it states clearly that the Commune was to be the political form of even the smallest country hamlet, and that in the rural districts the standing army was to be replaced by a national militia, with an extremely short term of service. The rural communes of every district were to administer their common affairs by an assembly of delegates in the central town, and these district assemblies were again to send delegates to the National Delegation in Paris, each delegate to be at any time revocable and bound by the *mandat imperatif* [formal instructions] of its constituents. *The few but important functions which still would remain for a central government were not to be suppressed, as has been intentionally misstated,*[18] *but were to be discharged by Communal, and therefore strictly responsible, agents.* ["The Class Struggles in France"; in McClellan, 1977: 542-543; emphasis added]

This last sentence is especially significant, for it reveals Marx's belief that even in communist society some minimal public functions would be necessary—although they would be executed in a fully accountable, nonbureaucratic fashion.

> When, in the course of development, class distinctions have disappeared, and all production has been concentrated in the hands of associated individuals, the public power will lose its political character. [*Communist Manifesto;* in McClellan, 1977: 237-238]

By this time the state would truly have withered away.

NOTES

1. Other examples mentioned by McClellan (1975) include the British Tudor government, which itself "created the conditions for the existence of British capitalism" (p. 63); the Asiatic mode of production, in which because of "the absence of private property in land, [the State] did not serve the interests of a particular class" (p. 64); and the modern absolute monarchy, which emerged when the old feudal classes were weak and dying.

2. Article published in the *New York Daily Tribune* (August 25). Kamenka (1983: cvi-cvii) comments that the *Tribune* articles are now believed to be principally the work of Engels; see Chapter 1.

3. Avineri (1968: 212-213) also points out that Marx opposed universal suffrage in Bismarckian Prussia on the grounds that it would promote instability and hence likely result in a rightist coup if used as a part of socialist strategy.

4. A summary of Marx's newly crystallized economic theory at the time of the *Manifesto* is contained in his 1847-1848 lectures to the Brussels' Workingman's Club, published in the *Neue Rheinische Zeitung* during April 1849 as "Wage-Labour and Capital," and reproduced in McClellan (1977: 248-268).

5. These include a series written for the *Neue Rheinische-Zeitung-Revue* in 1850, republished by Engels in 1895 under the title "The Class Struggles in France"; a pamphlet on Louis Napoleon Bonaparte's December 1851 seizure of power, published in a New York journal under the title *The Eighteenth Brumaire of Louis Bonaparte;* several 1851 articles for the *New York Daily Tribune* on the German workers' abortive uprisings, republished in 1896 under the title *Revolution and Counter-Revolution in Germany* (commissioned for Marx but actually written primarily by Engels, with Marx's approval); and finally an 1871 statement for the General Council of the International concerning the Paris Commune, published under the title "The Civil War in France." See Chapter 1 for a more detailed chronology.

6. The French uprisings sparked similar outbursts in Germany and Hungary, and throughout the Austrian Empire. In Germany a Constitutional Monarchy (rather than a republican form of government) was created, with the king of Prussia granted rule over an all-German state.

7. This refers, of course, to the economic crises of 1845-1847. In *The Eighteenth Brumaire* (in McClellan, 1977: 308), Marx had employed his economic framework to analyze the general economic cycle, over which he superimposed the economic conditions unique to France:

Apart from these special circumstances [partial failure of the cotton crop; fluctuations in the price of cotton, wool, and silk], the aparent crisis of 1851 was nothing else but the halt which overproduction and overspeculation invariably make in describing the industrial cycle, before they summon all their strength in order to feverishly rush through the final phase of this cycle and arrive once more at their starting-point, the general trade crisis . . . besides the general crisis, France goes through national trade crises of her own, which are nevertheless determined and conditioned far more by the general state of the world market than by French local influences.

8. Avineri's (1968: 218) conclusions concerning Marx's position on the use of violence appears to turn Marx into a pacifist: "One can summarize Marx's position by saying that for Marx physical power will either fail or prove to be superfluous." A more balanced assessment would suggest that Marx was agnostic on the use of violence. While he condemned its use under certain circumstances and troubled about its potentially adverse consequences, he did not issue a blanket condemnation; it was not Marx's style to draw universal conclusions of this sort.

9. Engels later commented, "History has proved us, and all who thought like us, wrong" (in Zeitlin, 1967: 142).

10. "This discipline will become superfluous under a social system in which the labourers work for their own account" (*Capital,* Volume 3: 83).

11. Marx's belief in the possibility of unalienated physical labor can nonetheless still be found even in his latest writings. In his 1875 *Critique of the Gotha Program,* for example, he comments that with the abolition of the division of labor (and particularly between mental and physical labor), "labour has become not only a means of life but life's prime want" (in McClellan, 1977: 569).

12. Marx comments in Volume 1 of *Capital* that even though the abolition of capitalism would greatly reduce the length of the working day, there would simultaneously be pressures to extend it—both "because the notion of 'means of subsistence' would considerably expand, and the labourer would lay claim to an altogether different standard of life" (p. 530), and because of the need to devote labor-time to capital accumulation (as well as immediate consumption).

13. Hence Marx's condemnation of "the asses, Bakunin and Cluseret," for their "most foolish decrees on the abolition de l'etat and similar nonsense" on behalf of the International during the Paris Commune (reproduced in Avineri, 1968: 208). As an anarchist, Bakunin opposed the state per se, while Marx believed it was suicidal to seek to abolish the state before conditions were ripe.

14. The actual phrase was first used by Marx in a March 5, 1852, letter to Joseph Weydemeyer; he also used it in the 1875 *Critique of the Gotha Program.*

15. Other provisions included a progressive income tax, the abolition of inheritance, the confiscation of rebel and emigrant property, the establishment of industrial work forces, the industrialization of agriculture, and free public education (see *Communist Manifesto;* in McClellan, 1977: 237).

16. As noted above, a more peaceful transition was still regarded as possible where permitted by nominally democratic institutions.

17. Engels, in his twentieth- (1891) anniversary introduction to "The Civil War in France," asked, "Do you want to know what this dictatorship looks like? Look at the Paris Commune. That was the Dictatorship of the Proletariat" (reproduced in Zeitlin, 1967: 77).

18. A reference to Bakunin's call for the complete abolition of the state.

PART III
Conclusion: The Dialectic of Structure and Action

7

Concluding Thoughts

We saw in Chapter 4 that Marx's earliest writings utilized critique to reveal the economic and social circumstances that prevent people from realizing their full potential. Marx's concern with understanding contemporary society led him to the intensive study of capitalist economics and politics, and eventually to the general theory of structured economic instability reviewed in Chapter 5. Although Marx never abandoned critique, in his mature writings he did place far greater emphasis on the concrete analysis of economic and political institutions. We are now in a position to return to the central problems with which we began: Marx's attempt to reconcile scientific determinism with philosophy's age-old concern for human freedom; the related question of the relationship between law and tendency; and the nature of Marx's version of social science.

STRUCTURE AND ACTION

In his substantive analysis, Marx did not treat human beings as blindly following universal laws that lead to predictable outcomes; he was not developing a social physics. Rather, in his actual account of the workings of capitalism Marx advanced the position that while the structures of competitive capitalism impose certain requirements on economic actors, those requirements are not determinant. Rather, the structures themselves constitute the often contradictory resources for human action, action that then leads to outcomes—some anticipated, some not—that both reproduce and undermine the structures themselves, creating new opportunities for action in the process.

Marx thus views society as consisting of a complex of relatively persisting structures, in which the economy is ultimately the most influential in determining the relative importance of other social, political, and ideological institutions. The economy enjoys this privileged position simply because in all societies to date economic problems are fundamental: People must be provided with a minimal level of subsistence if they (and society) are to biologically and socially reproduce themselves.

Throughout his writings Marx focused primarily on the economy, and almost exclusively so in his more mature theoretical works. He never lived to complete his projected writings on the polity, religion, ideology, and other social institutions; he never developed an explicit theory of how noneconomic structures function. He offers no noneconomic parallels for the labor theory of value and the concept of surplus labor value, ideas that provide the foundation for his theory of economic contradiction and crisis (Chapter 5). As a result, Marxist theories of the polity and ideology remain underdeveloped relative to Marxist economic theory.

Marx characterizes societies as alternating between periods of crisis and normality, primarily as the result of contradictions that arise within the economy. By "contradiction" Marx means contradictory economic system requirements—that is, conflicting demands placed on economic actors whose rational behavior will then undermine the economy itself. For example, capitalists are under powerful pressures to cut costs if they wish to survive in a competitive environment. This leads individual capitalists to adopt labor-saving technological innovations that—across the entire economy—result in increasing automation, the systematic impoverishment of labor, and ultimately a loss of market demand for the goods that are produced. This, in turn, leads to crises of overproduction and underconsumption. Furthermore, the impoverishment of labor undermines legitimacy and leads to social unrest, further destabilizing the system.

When economic contradictions occur they may be deflected to noneconomic social structures and thereby diffused—as when working-class demands for economic improvements lead to new government bureaucracies, co-opted leadership, and symbolic but empty victories (see Piven and Cloward, 1977). Or they may accumulate and eventually lead to an economic crisis. Such crises provide major occasions for organized political practice (class struggle), not only because they represent a real deterioration in the material conditions of life for large numbers of people, but also because they are crucial in revealing the underlying structural mechanisms of society.

So long as the economy is running smoothly, people will tend to regard the present state of affairs as "normal." Because society is operating with lawlike regularity and people are not forced by turbulent conditions to question its norms, the social world is reified as natural; people become "cheerful robots" (Mills, 1959: 171), relatively predictable in their behavior and attitudes. When an economic crisis occurs, however, people are more willing to confront their beliefs and assumptions. The crisis in the economic structure can lead to political and ideological crises as well, such as legitimation crises (Habermas, 1976) that render governance difficult or impossible. The underlying structures of society—hitherto hidden from view, and therefore known only as a result of (Marxist) theory—are now revealed to all who care to see. In Marx's view, ideological reformulation may follow a crisis, depending on the stage of class struggle: Efforts will be made to rationalize or explain the crisis in ways compatible with the interests of the classes and subclasses involved. The extent to which the crisis results in a rethinking of ideological beliefs along more "scientific" (that is, in Marx's view, his own) lines will depend on the strength and discipline of the Communist Party.

Crisis thus paves the way for dereification, and makes possible conscious, "scientifically" based action. If action is premature or adventurist, it is likely to fail, leaving a wake of violence and terror. If it is timidly aimed at superficial events rather than the underlying structures, the crisis will be diffused, the underlying conditions temporarily corrected, and the veils of reification will again fall—although in Marx's view the working class will hopefully have learned something in the process, and so will act with greater effectiveness when the next crisis comes.

For revolutionary social change to occur, action must be directed at the underlying structural sources of the crisis. This can occur only if action is guided by correct theoretical understanding, which enables fundamental structural instabilities to be distinguished from their superficial manifestations. In other words, it is crucial to "scientifically" distinguish revolutionary from reformist political practice. Marx's

Concluding Thoughts   141

acerbic writing style suggests that such distinctions are readily made; history, unfortunately, offers little reason for confidence that this is the case. During times of protracted economic crisis there are always numerous revolutionary organizations with bonafide Marxist credentials, all of which claim to have an exclusive line on scientific truth. Their differences are seldom settled through open scientific discourse.

It is important to bear in mind that structural conditions are conceived by Marx as socially accomplished rather than naturalistically given, however much they may be perceived otherwise during nonrevolutionary times. Even though he regards structures as humanly constituted, however, Marx also views them as strong short-run constraints on human action and perceptions. As he notes in the preface to the first German edition of *Capital* (in McClellan, 1977: 417, emphasis added),

> I paint the capitalist and the landlord in no sense *couleur de rose*. But here individuals are dealt with only insofar as they are the personification of economic categories, embodiments of particular class relations and class interests. My standpoint, from which the economic formation of society is viewed as a process of natural history, *can less than any other make the individual responsible for the relations whose creature he socially remains,* however much he may subjectively rise above them.

In this strongly sociological statement, all people—even the wealthy and powerful—are regarded as prisoners of their social roles, which are themselves largely shaped by the requirements of the social system. During times of crisis, the range of freedom may be greatly extended—permitting, for example, large and powerful capitalists to acquire more marginal enterprises, thereby reducing the competitive pressures that constrain them. Following a crisis, the range of action may again become restricted, although under a somewhat different set of structural constraints, such as those of monopoly (rather than competitive) capitalism. During periods of particularly acute crisis, a great many restrictions on action may be relaxed; during such times revolutions occur.

LAW AND TENDENCY

Marx's "laws" are theoretical statements concerning developmental structural tendencies within the capitalist economy. They follow from his analysis of the economic system requirements of the capitalist mode of production, and are employed to reveal structured instabilities or contradictions the eventual working out of which depends on the stage of class struggle. Capitalism, when conceived as a closed economic system, entails contradictory elements that work to undermine the system itself despite the intentions (and, indeed, even awareness) of its ruling class. As we saw in Chapter 5, Marx seeks to demonstrate that the logic of production entails both cyclical and long-term erosion of profitability: Rational profit-maximizing behavior on the part of individual capitalists spells long-term disaster for capitalists as a class. According to Marx, such contradictions are an inevitable feature of production in all societies in which the surplus produced by one class is appropriated by another. Since one result of such contradictions is a tendency toward recurrent economic crises, the resolution of contradictions cannot be predicted; final outcomes depend on the action taken by the principal classes involved in the production process.

In other words, Marx's "laws" are not predictive in the ordinary sense of that term: They rather describe a field of forces operating in a structured environment on classes of actors, whose concerted action—if informed by correct theory—can alter the field itself. A properly organized and politically conscious working class has the potential of altering the very structures that constrain them, providing new opportunities for class-conscious action aimed at directing the course of history. Ultimately, Marx believed, the "laws" of capitalist economics can be overturned altogether, through the creation of a communally run, classless society.

In *Capital,* Marx often presents lawful statements as formal (algebraic) equations. Such equations have a uniquely hybrid status in his theory: They permit the deduction of logical outcomes of economic forces, while at the same time denoting the locus of political actions constrained by (and in turn acting back upon) those very forces. In other words, his key conceptual building blocks—V, C, and S—cannot be regarded as independent variables in a predictive equation. Rather, they are at once analytic categories for understanding structural relationships and tendencies, and political indicators of the degree of the class struggle. Let us briefly illustrate this by returning to the example of the declining rate of profit. We have previously noted (in Chapter 5) that this is one of the more deterministic aspects of Marx's crisis theory; yet I believe that even in this case Marx's theory is one of structural constraint and enablement, rather than one of "natural laws of [society's] movement" (Preface to *Capital,* Volume 1; in McClellan, 1977: 417). In this example, the principal structures of analytic interest are economic: the factory system, organized in such a way that labor produces for the profit of the owners of capital; a market economy, in which production is for individual profit rather than the common good; and overall economic organization predicated on competition among workers for jobs and capitalists for markets rather than on coordination and central social planning. These structures are organized neither as a collection of random or accidentally related elements, nor as a closed system in which all parts possess causally determinate relationships with all others. Rather, the structures are conceived dialectically as reciprocally influencing one another in an ongoing process. Consider equations 4 and 5 from Chapter 5:

$$P = S/(C + V) \qquad [4]$$

$$P = S'^{*}(1 - Q) \qquad [5]$$

These equations tell us a number of things about the rate of profit. First, they show that the rate of profit is defined as consisting of specified relationships between constant capital, variable capital, and surplus value. Given values for C, V, and S, the rate of profit is directly determined by the equations, which serve as formal representations of an empirical event. Like all such representations, they have the property of abstracting away from concrete phenomena to highly simplified mathematical models. This, in turn, permits logical deductions to be drawn according to standard mathematical rules.

Equations 4 and 5 not only define the rate of profit; they are also embedded within an economic theory that suggests developmental tendencies among the elements of the equations, and hence possible future values of the rate of profit. Since Marx defines the rate of profit as directly proportional to the mass of surplus value and inversely proportional to the total capital advanced, it follows that to the extent that living labor (V) is replaced by past or dead labor in the form of machinery (C), surplus value and hence profits will dry up, at least insofar as increases in the rate of surplus value (S') prove inadequate to offset the necessarily rising organic composition (Q). In other words, the several terms of equations 4 and 5 are linked together within a coherent theoretical framework that makes it possible to deduce certain outcomes among them.

At these first two levels there is no difference between Marx's method and ւne methods conventionally associated with the more empiricist versions of social science. The difference emerges when one asks the question, "Is a rising organic composition in fact likely actually to outstrip a rising rate of surplus value?" The answer to this question is not mathematically deducible from the equations themselves, nor can it be derived from any other equations in Marx's theory. Rather, the answer will depend on actions among conscious human agents—in particular, the state of the class struggle between labor and capital. The locus of this struggle, just like the key economic variables, is denoted by S, V, and C. Let us take up each of these elements in turn.

Surplus value (S), for example, is the arena of the struggle between workers and capital over the duration of the working day and the intensity of the labor process. That is why Marx, after introducing the concepts of C, V, and S in *Capital,* immediately proceeds to a discussion of the concept of absolute surplus value and a lengthy historical exposition of concrete struggles over the length of the working day in England. That is also why he follows the chapter on absolute surplus value with one on relative surplus value and the intensity of the labor process in modern industry. The outcome of the class struggle over the disposition of the surplus cannot be derived simply from the theoretical conceptualization of capitalist production, although it is certainly shaped by the conditions of production—for example, workers' concentration in factories, which "replaces the isolation of the labourers, due to competition, by their revolutionary combination, due to association" (*Communist Manifesto;* in McClellan, 1977: 231). Rather, the outcome of that struggle, which occurs within the framework of structural conditions represented by the equations, is ultimately a product of concrete historical circumstances. These include the degree of working-class consciousness and political mobilization, the level of theoretical understanding on the part of the working class and its leaders, the ability of capital to extract surplus from foreign workers to the detriment of workers at home, and the extent to which monopolization alters the ability of major capitalists to amass large surpluses while retarding the increase of the organic composition of capital.

Variable capital (V) draws our attention to another set of struggles: those having to do with the wage bill and workers' subsistence. The numerical values taken on by this term will reflect the degree to which labor is able to resist capital's efforts to depress its value. These efforts, as we have seen, take the form of cheapening the means of subsistence, reducing all labor to unskilled detail labor (and hence reducing the costs of subsistence by making it possible for all members of the family to work), depressing wages below their value, and shifting production to colonies with a ready source of cheap labor. Labor's success in this struggle depends, in turn, on its degree of organization and militancy. It depends upon the strength of unions, the access of the labor organizations to parliamentary institutions, and the degree of internationalization of the working-class movement (which means, for

Marx, the strength of the Communist Party). It also depends on the degree of tolerance for organized labor on the part of capital: whether or not labor is ruthlessly suppressed, accepted as a legitimate political actor, or even co-opted into political leadership. It is precisely because none of these conditions follows automatically from economic circumstances that Marx stressed the theoretical importance of organizing workers under the aegis of a unified, international socialist party—and then devoted much of his political life to doing so.

The final set of struggles, those having to do with constant capital (C), reflect in part technological conditions (e.g., the extent to which labor-saving technologies are capital-saving as well), in part the organization of production (e.g., the rate of capital turnover), and in part the ability of capitalists to extend capitalist economic relations abroad (e.g., foreign investment, which permits the importation of cheap raw materials and machinery produced with low-paid foreign labor). The value of constant capital in Marx's equations also reflects the socio-political organization of capitalists as a class—the intensity of competition individual capitalists, their degree of centralization and co-operation, and the extent of their political and ideological power in society. These conditions, in turn, draw attention to the role of the state in securing capitalist economic relations—the degree to which it actively serves as a "committee for managing the common affairs of the whole bourgeoisie," as Marx asserts in the *Communist Manifesto* (in McClellan, 1977: 223). Again, such circumstances cannot be directly predicted on the basis of underlying economic conditions, although the latter do limit and shape the range of possible choices.

The struggle over the disposition of the surplus, workers' share in output, and capitalists' initial control over the economic, political, and ideological spheres are different aspects of the class struggle. That struggle is not purely economic, although it depends to a large extent on economic conditions. The class struggle, as seen by Marx, also moves at the political and cultural levels. The possibilities of delegitimation of the state and dereification of both popular and scientific culture flow from economic struggles, and shape those struggles. That is why "theory, too, will become material force as soon as it has seized the masses" (*Critique of Hegel's Philosophy of Right;* in McClellan, 1977: 69).

There is nothing automatic about the processes of social change. This is true of the "stages of societal development" often attributed to Marx, as well as of more historically bounded economic "laws" such as those concerning the falling rate of profit. The movement of concrete societies occurs within well-defined structural limits, which themselves provide the resources for action aimed at structural transformation. The limits can thus be changed; the relationships among parameters themselves can change apart from their hypothesized economic connections within formal equations. This is because C, V, and S, while serving as economic parameters, are simultaneously conceptualized by Marx as signifying social relations. Social relations can be altered, within bounds—and thereby the bounds themselves can be altered. The bounds are, for Marx, first and foremost the structural constraints on economic production. These constraints generate contradictory requirements that pose problems for the system as a whole, while at the same time setting limits to the probable solutions of those problems. The solutions to the problems of competitive capitalism historically involved the emergence of monopoly capitalism, economic imperialism, and extensive state intervention. These solutions, in turn, engender their own structural frameworks, replete with their own historically specific contradictions demanding new solutions if the stability of the system is to be maintained (see Baran and Sweezy, 1966; Mattick, 1969; Wright, 1975; O'Connor, 1973). The likelihood and efficacy of any solution depend, on the one hand, on the legitimacy accorded to state intervention, and on class consciousness on the other. Legitimation crises, the collapse of ideology, and class struggle may grow out of adverse economic conditions, or out of equally adverse solutions to such conditions, but they are not reducible to economic factors.

The future cannot be predicted from Marx's theory. It only can be shaped, with effectiveness depending on the extent to which actions are based on an adequate theoretical understanding. Marxist theory is a theory of structural constraints and probable tendencies, both of which are themselves shaped and modified by human activity.

THE NATURE OF SCIENTIFIC UNDERSTANDING

Let us conclude with some brief observations concerning Marx's understanding of science. As noted in Chapter 5, while Marx often writes as if he were working within what would today be termed the *natural science model,* his actual practice belies such a self-under-standing. Marx in fact rejects pure empiricism, arguing instead that theory is essential in constituting our understanding of reality. Marx does not share the empiricist belief that the future can be predicted on the basis of intractable laws. Rather, he assumes that human con-sciousness and external reality act upon one another in an ongoing dialectic. While social structures may often be experienced as "social facts" in the Durkheimian sense of externality and constraint, Marx does not thereby conclude that they are in fact external realities somehow impervious to change. Rather, structures are regarded as both resource for—and outcome of—human agency, and are ultimately realized only as the result of social practices (Giddens, 1984: 16-28).

It is true that social structures often appear to be hidden from view, operating behind our backs as a sort of invisible but potent reality. But while we may sometimes assume that there is an underlying structural reality determining both our behavior and our perceptions, such an assumption is both misleading and dangerous: misleading because it renders us the creatures of blind historical forces, and dangerous because it lends itself to dogmatic claims on the part of "scientific experts" who claim to have a privileged understanding of "reality." Structures are invisible because they exist for us only as theoretical constructs. We do not "see" them, because they do not simply "exist"; rather, they can be identified only with the aid of theory. While we may assume the existence of real structures as the ultimate ground of such theoretical labor, we do so instrumentally—to ensure a concern with some form of objective empirical confirmation—rather than dogmatically. Structures are both revealed and disguised through their surface effects; only an adequate theory can provide a provisional understanding of their nature and operation.

Marx's theory is like any other in that its central concepts and methodological self-understandings reflect in part the conventions that govern the community of (Marxist) theorists. Kuhn's (1970) sociology of scientific practice is certainly no less applicable to Marxism than it is to physics or chemistry. While this position seems to be the most defensible one in light of the history of the philosophy of science over the past 70 years (Suppe, 1974), it is arguable on purely practical grounds as well: Surely it is better to err on the side of humility than dogmatism, if one assumes that the existing state of any would-be social science is far from perfect. Marxism is always an "applied science" in that it regards theory and practice as mutually constitutive. In the words of Marx's last thesis on Feuerbach—engraved on his tombstone—"philosophers have only interpreted the world, in various ways; the point is to change it." When one seeks to change the world armed with a theory mantled with the legitimacy of science, the political and human costs of theoretical error can be high indeed. A skeptical attitude toward all proffered claims to truth is not only in the best tradition of scientific inquiry; it is a partial safeguard against potential political disaster.

Throughout his lifetime Marx was engaged in an unremitting assault on all forms of reification, including and in particular the uncritical acceptance of supposedly scientific authority. Marxism can grow only to the extent that it steadfastly refuses to see itself as exempt from this critical spirit.

References

Works by Marx and Engels Cited or Mentioned in the Text

Marx, Karl

1837
Letter to his father, November 10 (in McClellan, 1977: 5-10)

1841
"The Difference Between the Democritean and Epicurean Philosophy of Nature" (complete translation in *Karl Marx-Frederick Engels: Collected Works,* Vol. I: 25-107. New York: International Publishers, 1975; excerpted in McClellan, 1977: 11-16)

1843
"Contribution to the Critique of Hegel's 'Philosophy of law'" (complete translation in *Karl Marx-Frederick Engels: Collected Works,* Vol. III: 3-129. New York: International Publishers, 1975; excerpted in McClellan, 1977: 26-35, under the title, "Critique of Hegel's 'Philosophy of Right'")
"On the Jewish Question" (complete translation in *Karl Marx-Frederick Engels:Collected Works,* Vol. III: 146-174. New York: International Publishers, 1975; excerpted in McClellan, 1977: 39-62)
September letter to Arnold Ruge (complete translation in *Karl Marx-Frederick Engels: Collected Works,* Vol. III: 141-145. New York: International Publishers, 1975; excerpted in Tucker, 1972: 7-10)

1843-44
"Contribution to the Critique of Hegel's 'Philosophy of Law': Introduction" (complete translation in *Karl Marx-Frederick Engels: Collected Works,* Vol. III pp. 175-187. New York: International Publishers, 1975; excerpted in McClellan, 1977: 63-74, under the title, "Towards a Critique of Hegel's 'Philosophy of Right': Introduction")

1844
Economic and Philosophical Manuscripts (complete translation in L. Easton and K. Guddatt, eds., *Writings of the Young Marx on Philosophy and Society.* New York, 1967; excerpted in McClellan, 1977: 75-112)

1845
(with Engels) *The Holy Family* (complete translation in R. Dixon, trans., *The Holy Family.* Moscow, 1956; excerpted in McClellan, 1977: 131-155)

Theses on Feuerbach (in McClellan, 1977: 156-158)

1845-6
(with Engels) *The German Ideology* (complete translation of Vol. I in Marx and Engels, *The German Ideology*. Moscow: Progress Publishers, 1964; excerpted in McClellan, 1977: 159-191)

1847
The Poverty of Philosophy (complete translation in Karl Marx, *The Poverty of Philosophy*. Moscow: Progress Publishers, n.d.; excerpted in McClellan, 1977: 195-215)

1848
(with Engels) *Communist Manifesto* (in McClellan, 1977: 221-247)

1849
"Wage-Labour and Capital" (in McClellan, 1977: 248-268)

1850
The Class Struggles in France (excerpted in McClellan, 1977: 286-297)

1851-1852
Revolution and Counter-Revolution in Germany. London: E.M. Aveling, 1896

1852
"The Chartists" (*New York Daily Tribune*, August 25; excerpted in Avineri, 1968: 214)
(March 5) letter to Joseph Weydemeyer (excerpted in McClellan, 1977: 341)
"The Eighteenth Brumaire of Louis Bonaparte" (in McClellan, 1977: 300-325)

1856
Revelations of the Diplomatic History of the 18th Century. London: E.M. Aveling, 1899

1857-8
Grundrisse der Kritik der Politischen Okonomie (complete translation in Martin Nicolaus, *Karl Marx: Grundrisse*. New York: Vintage, 1973)

1859
Preface to *A Critique of Political Economy* (excerpted in McClellan, 1977: 388-391)

1860
Herr Vogt, London, 1860

1865
Value, Price, and Profit. London: E.M. Aveling, 1898 (excerpted in Kamenka, 1983: 394-432)
"Confessions of Marx" (in Kamenka, 1983: 53)

1867
Capital, Vol. 1: A Critique of Political Economy. New York: International Publishers, 1967a (excerpted in McClellan, 1977: 413-488)

1867-1887
Theories of Surplus Value (unpublished notes). Moscow: Progress Publishers, 3 volumes issued in 1963, 1968, and 1971 (excerpted in McClellan, 1977: 393-414)

1871
"The Civil War in France" (Karl Marx and Frederick Engels, *Selected Works* (2 volumes).
Moscow: Progress Publishers, 1935; excerpted in McClellan, 1977: 539-558)
Letter to Friedrich Bolte, Secretary of the American Federal Council of the International,
November 23 (excerpted in McClellan, 1977: 587-589)
(April 12) letter to Ludwig Kugelman (excerpted in McClellan, 1977: 592-593)

1872
September 18 speech at the Hague Congress of the International (in H. Gerth, ed., 1958,
The First International: Minutes of the Hague Conference of 1872. Madison:
University of Wisconsin Press)

1875
Critique of the Gotha Program (in Tucker, 1972: 382-398)

1877
"Aus der 'Kritischen Geschichte'"; became chapter 10 of Engels's *Anti-Duhring* (see
below)

1880
Letter to Henry M. Hyndman, founder of the Social Democratic Federation, December 8
(reproduced in H. M. Hyndman, 1911, The Record of an Adventurous Life. London)
"Enquete ouvriere" (complete translation in T. Bottomore and M. Rubel, eds., 1956, Karl
Marx: Selected Writings in Sociology and Social Philosophy. London: Watts)

1881
March 8 letter to the Russian socialist Vera Zasulich (excerpted in McClellan, 1977:
576-580)

1884
Capital, Vol. 2: The Process of Circulation of Capital. New York: International
Publishers, 1967b

1885
Capital, Vol. 3: The Process of Capitalist Production as a Whole. New York: International
Publishers, 1967c (excerpted in McClellan, 1977: 488-507)

1898
Value, Price, and Profit. London: Aveling

Engels, Frederick

1843
Outlines of a Critique of Political Economy (complete translation in *Karl Marx-Frederick
Engels: Collected Works,* Vol. III: 418-443. New York: International Publishers, 1975)

1844
The Condition of the Working Class in England. New York: Penguin Classics, 1987

1876
Dialectics of Nature. Moscow: Foreign Languages Publishing House, 1954

1878
Anti-Duhring: Herr Eugen Duhring's Revolution in Science. New York: International
Publishers, (1939)

1884
"Origins of the Family, Private Property, and the State," in *Marx and Engels: Selected
Works,* New York: International, 1968

1890
September 21, letter to J. Bloch (in Tucker, 1972: 640-647)

Principal Collected Works of Marx and Engels

1927-1935
Marx-Engels Gesamtausgabe (MEGA), Moscow: Marx-Engels Institute

1957-1968
Marx-Engels Werke (40 volumes). Berlin

1975-
Karl Marx-Frederick Engels: Collected Works (50 volumes projected; 30 published as of
1987). New York: International Publishers (simultaneously with Lawrence and
Wishart Ltd., London, and Progress Publishers, Moscow)

Secondary Sources Cited

ALTHUSSER, L. (1969) For Marx. London: Penguin.
ANDERSON, P. (1974a) Lineages of the Absolutist State. London: New Left.
ANDERSON, P. (1974b) Passages From Antiquity to Feudalism. London: New Left.
APPELBAUM, R. P. (1978a) "Marx's theory of the falling rate of profit." American
Sociological Review 43 (February): 67-80.
APPELBAUM, R. P. (1978b) "Marxist method: structural constraints and social praxis."
American Sociologist 13 (February): 73-81.
APPELBAUM, R. P. (1979) "Born-again functionalism? A reconsideration of Althusser's
structuralism." Insurgent Sociologist 9 (1): 18-33.
APPELBAUM, R. P. and H. CHOTINER (1979) "Science, philosophy and dialectics in
Marxist method." Socialist Review 9 (4): 71-108.
AVINERI, S. (1968) The Social and Political Thought of Karl Marx. Cambridge:
Cambridge University Press.
BALL, T. and J. FARR [eds.] (1984) After Marx. Cambridge: Cambridge University
Press.
BARAN, P. and P. SWEEZY (1966) Monopoly Capital. New York: Monthly Review.
BERLIN, I. (1978) Karl Marx: His Life and Environment (4th ed.). New York: Oxford
University Press. .
BERNSTEIN, R. J. (1971) Praxis and Action. Philadelphia: University of Pennsylvania
Press.
BLOCH, M. (1966) French Rural History. Berkeley: University of California Press.
BLOCH, M. (1967) Land and Work in Medieval Europe. London: Routledge & Kegan
Paul.

BRAVERMAN, H. (1974) Labor and Monopoly Capital. New York: Monthly Review.

BRENNER, R. (1976) "Agrarian class structure and economic development in pre-industrial Europe." Past and Present 70: 30-75.

BURGER, T. (1976) Max Weber's Theory of Concept Formation: History, Laws, and Ideal Types. Durham, NC: Duke University Press.

CARVER, T. (1981) Engels. New York: Hill & Wang.

CARVER, T. (1982) Marx's Social Theory. New York: Oxford University Press.

COGOY, M. (1973) "The fall of the rate of profit and the theory of accumulation: a reply to Paul Sweezy." Bulletin of the Conference of Socialist Economists (winter): 52-67.

COHEN, G. A. (1978) Karl Marx's Theory of History: A Defense. Princeton: Princeton University Press.

COLLETTI, L. (1971) "The Marxism of the Second International." Telos 8 (summer): 84-91.

COSER, L. A. (1977) Masters of Sociological Thought (2nd ed.). New York: Harcourt Brace Jovanovich.

FEUER, L. (1959) Marx & Engels: Basic Writings on Politics and Philosophy. New York: Doubleday Anchor.

FEUERBACH, L. (1957) The Essence of Christianity. (1881) New York: Harper.

FROMM, E. (1963) Marx's Concept of Man. New York: Frederick Ungar.

GARAUDY, R. (1967) Karl Marx: The Evolution of his Thought. New York: International Publishers.

GIDDENS, A. (1979) Central Problems in Social Theory: Action, Structure, and Contradiction in Social Analysis. Berkeley: University of California Press.

GIDDENS, A. (1981) A Contemporary Critique of Historical Materialism. Berkeley: University of California Press.

GIDDENS, A. (1984) The Constitution of Society. Berkeley: University of California Press.

GOTTHEIL, F. M. (1966) Marx's Economic Predictions. Evanston, IL: Northwestern University Press.

GOULDNER, A. (1980) The Two Marxisms. New York: Oxford University Press.

HABERMAS, J. (1971) Knowledge and Human Interests. Boston: Beacon.

HABERMAS, J. (1975) "The place of philosophy in Marxism." Insurgent Sociologist 5 (2): 41-48.

HABERMAS, J. (1976) Legitimation Crisis. London: Heinemann.

HARTNACK, J. (1967) Kant's Theory of Knowledge. New York: Harcourt, Brace, & World.

HELD, D. (1980) Introduction to Critical Theory: Horkheimer to Habermas. Berkeley: University of California Press.

HOWARD, D. and K. E. KLARE (1972) The Unknown Dimension: European Marxism Since Lenin. New York: Basic Books.

HUME, D. (1968a) "An enquiry into human understanding," in A. J. Ayer and R. Winch (eds.) British Empirical Philosophers. (1748) New York: Simon & Schuster.

HUME, D. (1968b) "A treatise concerning human nature," in A. J. Ayer and R. Winch (eds.) British Empirical Philosophers. (1739-1740) New York: Simon & Schuster.

HYLAN, D. A. (1973) The Origins of Philosophy: Its Rise in Myth and the Pre-Socratics. New York: Putnam's.

JAY, M. (1973) The Dialectical Imagination: A History of the Frankfurt School and the Institute of Social Research, 1923-1950. Boston: Little, Brown.

JESSOP, R. (1982) The Capitalist State: Marxist Theories and Methods. New York: New York University Press.

KAMENKA, E. (1983) The Portable Karl Marx. New York: Viking Penguin.

KEAT, R. and J. URRY (1975) Social Theory as Science. London: Routledge & Kegan Paul.

KUHN, T. (1970) The Structure of Scientific Revolutions. Chicago: University of Chicago Press.

LACLAU, E. (1977) Politics and Ideology in Marxist Theory. Atlantic Highlands, NJ: Humanities.

LEISS, W. (1974) The Domination of Nature. Boston: Beacon.

LENIN, V. I. (1968) "'Left-wing' communism: an infantile disorder," in J. E. O'Connor (ed.) Lenin on Politics and Revolution. (1920) New York: Pegasus.

LENIN, V. I. (1971) Lenin: Selected Works in One Volume. New York: International.

LENIN, V. I. (1972) Materialism and Empirio-Criticism. (1927) New York: International Publishers.

LITTLE, D. (1986) The Scientific Marx. Minneapolis: University of Minnesota Press.

LUKACS, G. (1971a) History and Class Consciousness: Studies in Marxist Dialectics. Cambridge: MIT Press.

LUKACS, G. (1971b) "Reification and the consciousness of the proletariat," in History and Class Consciousness: Studies in Marxist Dialectics. Cambridge: MIT Press.

LUKACS, G. (1971c) "What is orthodox Marxism?" in History and Class Consciousness: Studies in Marxist Dialectics. Cambridge: MIT Press.

MANDEL, E. (1968) Marxist Economic Theory (2 volumes). New York: Monthly Review.

MANDEL, E. (1970) An Introduction to Marxist Economic Theory. New York: Pathfinder.

MARCUSE, H. (1955) Eros and Civilization: A Philosophical Inquiry Into Freud. Boston: Beacon.

MARCUSE, H. (1964) One-Dimensional Man. Boston: Beacon.

MARCUSE, H. (1969) Reason and Revolution: Hegel and the Rise of Social Theory. Boston: Beacon.

MATTICK, P. (1969) Marx and Keynes: The Limits of the Mixed Economy. Boston: Porter Sargent.

McCLELLAN, D. (1969) The Young Hegelians and Karl Marx. London: Macmillan.

McCLELLAN, D. (1975) Karl Marx. New York: Viking Press.

McCLELLAN, D. (1977) Karl Marx: Selected Writings. London: Oxford.

McMURTRY, J. (1977) The Structure of Marx's World-View. Princeton: Princeton University Press.

MEPHAM, J. and D.-H. RUBEN [eds.] (1979) Issues in Marxist Philosophy. Atlantic Highlands, NJ: Humanities.

MESZAROS, I. (1970) Marx's Theory of Alienation. London: Merlin.

MILIBAND, R. (1969) The State in Capitalist Society. New York: Basic Books.

MILIBAND, R. (1977) Marxism and Politics. New York: Oxford University Press.

MILIBAND, R. (1982) Capitalist Democracy in Britain. Oxford: Oxford University Press.

MILLS, C. W. (1959) The Sociological Imagination. New York: Oxford University Press.

MILLS, C. W. (1962) The Marxists. New York: Penguin.

MONTESQUIEU, C. (1962)The Spirit of the Laws. (1749) New York: Hafner.

MORISHIMA, M. (1973) Marx's Economics: A Dual Theory of Value and Growth. Cambridge: Cambridge University Press.

MOURELATOS, A.P.D. (1974) The Pre-Socratics: A Collection of Critical Essays. New York: Doubleday Anchor.

NICOLAIEVSKY, B. and O. MENCHEN-HELFEN (1936) Karl Marx: Man and Fighter. New York: Lippincott.

NICOLAUS, M. (1973) "Introduction," in Karl Marx: Grundrisse. New York: Vintage.

O'CONNOR, J. (1973) The Fiscal Crisis of the State. New York: St. Martin's.

OFFE, C. (1984) Contradictions of the Welfare State. Cambridge: MIT Press.

OGBURN, W. H. (1964) On Culture and Social Change. Chicago: University of Chicago Press.

OLLMAN, B. (1971) Alienation: Marx's Concept of Man in Capitalist Society. Cambridge: Cambridge University Press.

PADOVER, S. K. (1978) The Man Marx. New York: McGraw-Hill.

PARKINSON, G.H.R. [ed.] (1982) Marx and Marxisms. Cambridge: Cambridge University Press.

PIVEN, F. F. and R. CLOWARD (1977) Poor People's Movements: Why They Succeed, How They Fail. New York: Random House.

PLATO (1949) Timeaus (B. Jowett, trans.). New York: Liberal Arts.

POULANTZAS, N. (1975) Political Power and Social Classes. London: New Left.

RADIN, P. (1957) Primitive Man as Philosopher. New York: Dover.

ROEMER, J. (1981a) Analytical Foundations of Marxian Economic Theory. Cambridge: Cambridge University Press.

ROEMER, J. (1981b) "R. P. Wolff's reinterpretation of Marx's labor theory of value." Philosophy and Public Affairs 12: 70-83.

ROEMER, J. (1982a) A General Theory of Exploitation and Class. Cambridge, MA: Harvard University Press.

ROEMER, J. (1982b) "Methodological individualism and deductive Marxism." Theory and Society 11: 513-520.

ROEMER, J. (1982c) "New directions in the Marxian theory of exploitation." Politics and Society 11: 253-287.

ROEMER, J.(1982d) "Property relations vs. surplus value in the Marxian theory of exploitation." Philosophy and Public Affairs 11: 281-313.

RUBEN, D.-H. (1979) Marxism and Materialism (2nd ed.). Atlantic Highlands, NJ: Humanities.

SARTRE, J. P. (1971) "Replies to structuralism: an interview." Telos 9 (Fall): 110-116.

SAYER, D. (1979) Marx's Method. Atlantic Highlands, NJ: Humanities.

SHAW, W. (1978) Marx's Theory of History. Stanford: Stanford University Press.

SHUTZ, A. (1970) On Phenomenology and Social Relations. H. R. Wagner (ed.). Chicago: University of Chicago Press.

SINGER, P. (1980) Marx. Oxford: Oxford University Press.

SMITH, A. (1937) Wealth of Nations. New York: Modern Library.

STEEDMAN, I. (1977) Marx After Sraffa. London: New Left.

STEEDMAN, I. [ed.] (1981) The Value Controversy. London: New Left.

SWEEZY, P. M. (1942) The Theory of Capitalist Development. New York: Modern Reader.

SUPPE, F. (1974) "The search for philosophic understanding of scientific theories," pp. 3-241 in F. Suppe (ed.) The Structure of Scientific Theories. Urbana: University of Illinois Press.

SZYMANSKI, A. (1973) "Marxism and science." Insurgent Sociologist 3 (3): 25-38.

TUCKER, R. (1961) Philosophy and Myth in Karl Marx. Cambridge: Cambridge University Press.

TUCKER, R. (1972). The Marx-Engels Reader. New York: .W. W. Norton.

WILSON, E. (1940) To The Finland Station. New York: Harcourt Brace Jovanovich.
WOLFF, R. P. (1981) "A critique and reinterpretation of Marx's labor theory of value." Philosophy and Public Affairs 10: 89-120.
WOLFF, R. P. (1982) "Reply to Roemer." Philosophy and Public Affairs 12: 84-88.
WOLFF, R. P. (1984) Understanding Marx. Princeton: Princeton University Press.
WOOD, A. (1981) Karl Marx. London: Routledge & Kegan Paul.
WRIGHT, E. O. (1975) "An alternative perspective in the Marxist theory of accumulation and crisis." Insurgent Sociologist 6 (1): 5-39.
WRIGHT, E. O. (1978) Class, Crisis, and the State. London: Verso.
YAFFE, D. S. (1973) "The Marxian theory of crisis, capital, and the state." Economy and Society 2 (May): 186-232.
ZEITLIN, I. (1967) Marxism: A Re-Examination. New York: Van Nostrand Reinhold.
ZEITLIN, I. (1981) Capitalism and Modern Social Theory. Englewood Cliffs, NJ: Prentice-Hall.

Name Index

Subject Index

32-33; as science, 13-14, 15, 16n, 21, 38, 43, 45-47, 69-70, 83, 87-113, 138, 146-147; as Soviet orthodoxy, 10, 12, 13; as structuralism, 14, 70; "two Marxisms," 11-14, 16n; in the United States, 9-15; vision of the future, 16, 20, 32, 78, 111, 118, 129-136; vulgar, 10
Marxist theory of alienation, 10, 11, 14, 62, 70-74, 102, 115n, 131, 137n; fourfold nature of, 72-73, 75-76, 78, 95
Marxist theory of capitalist economics, 14, 27, 39, 65, 70, 74, 80-81, 90, 96-112, 121, 141; assumptions underlying, 99-101; crisis and instability in, 11, 13, 74, 96, 104-113, 115n, 118, 130, 139-142; profitability crises, 105, 106-109, 113, 115n, 116n, 142; profitability crises of the business cycle, 13, 97, 106-107, 111; profitability crises of the declining rate of profit, 107-109, 142-146; realization crises, 105, 109-112, 115n; realization crises from underconsumption, 109-111, 139; realization crises from disproportionality, 111-112
Marxist theory of concept formation: see Marxism, methodology
Marxist theory of consciousness, 74, 80-81, 83-84, 85n, 88, 90-92, 93, 124-125, 126-129, 144, 146
Marxist theory of human nature, 11, 71, 73-74, 76-77, 83, 93, 114n, 130-133
Marxist theory of labor process, 10-11, 43-44, 70-71, 73-74, 85n, 98, 103, 115n, 115n, 144
Marxist theory of politics, 13, 14, 16, 98-104, 105, 108, 117-136
Marxist theory of social change, 10, 11, 15, 88, 90, 95, 96, 97, 118, 126, 128, 140, 145
Marxist theory of the state, 14, 111, 117-124, 130-131, 133-136, 145, 146; abolition of, 133-136, 137n; dictatorship of the proletariat, 130-131, 133-134, 137n; as instrument of class domination, 117-119, 133, 145; legitimation of, 11, 107, 119, 139, 145-146; liberal democratic, 118, 128, 134, 136n, 144; relative autonomy of, 117-119
Mass production: see Production, mass
Material conditions, 91-92, 131
Materialism, 38-39, 43, 50-52, 53-54, 62, 83
Meaning, problem of, 114n
Means of production: see Production, means of
Mechanism, 51-52, 53-54, 91
Methodological holism, 54, 64-65
Methodological individualism, 54, 64
Methodenstreit, 114n
Mode of production: see Production, mode of
Monopoly, 107, 112, 119, 121, 129, 141, 144-146

Natural attitude, 48
Natural science model, 38-39, 42, 45-46, 62-63, 87-96, 112, 114n, 146

Negation, 59-60
Newtonianism, 53-54, 65
Object-subject relations: see Subject-object relations
Paris Commune: see France, Paris Commune
Peasantry, 122-124
Petty bourgeoisie, 122, 125, 134
Philosophes, 39, 63-64
Philosophic idealism: see Idealism
Philosophic materialism: see Materialism
Platonism, 49-50
Pluralism, 14, 118
Polarization: see Class struggle
Political economy, 16, 21, 37, 45, 46, 64-66, 70-71, 79, 81, 83, 90, 98, 101, 106
Population, 78-79, 110, 130
Positivism, 38, 47n, 80, 87, 89, 93
Poverty: see Labor, exploitation of
Praxis, 42, 43-45, 47n, 57, 97, 126
Predictability: see Determinism
Price, 65, 98
Production: cost of, 100, 109-110, 116n; forces of, 91, 93, 132; mass, 103, 115n; means of, 130-131; mode of, 88, 91, 93, 94, 95, 114nn, 141; over-, 110, 139; relations of, 91, 93, 146
Profitability: see Rate of profit
Profits, 102, 105, 106, 112, 116nn
Proletariat, 25, 26, 27, 73, 83, 84, 94-96, 97, 101, 103, 107, 109, 114n, 119, 120, 122-126, 131, 134, 135, 139, 140, 142-144; see also Marxist theory of the state, dictatorship of the proletariat
Property, 58, 62, 68n, 70-71, 92, 93, 94, 95, 114n, 130-131
Psychology: see Marxist theory of consciousness
Purposiveness: see Agency, human
Rate of profit, 85n; 101, 102, 104, 105, 116nn, 142-146
Rate of surplus value: see Labor, rate of surplus value of
Rationalism, 40, 41, 50, 56-57, 83
Reason, 40, 49-50, 58, 62, 83
Reflection theory, 92, 114n
Reforms, 107, 140
Reification, 12, 17n, 32-33, 41, 69-70, 75, 81, 83, 84, 85n, 90, 98, 140
Reign of Terror, 20
Relative surplus value: see Labor, surplus value of
Rents, 102-103
Revolution, 42, 64, 78, 83, 90, 94-96, 123, 124, 126-129, 140, 141, 144
Ruling class: see Class, ruling

Science: legitimating power of, 12, 96, 141, 147;
    philosophy of, 46-47, 147; as praxis, 45, 147;
    as productive force, 77-78, 133
Scientific management, 85n, 103
Scientific revolution, 38, 52-54
Scientism, 38, 39, 46, 87, 96-97
Social change: see Marxist theory of social
    change
Socialism, utopian, 22, 45-46
Socialist party, 9, 112
Socialist sectarianism, 127-128
Soviet Union, 9, 10, 12
Species-being: see Marxist theory of human
    nature
Structural constraint, 14, 16, 23, 24, 89, 97, 105,
    108, 111-112, 141-142, 145-146
Structuralism: see Marxism, as structuralism
Structuration: 14-15, 44-45, 139, 147
Structure, 14, 15, 16, 46, 138-141, 146-147; duality
    of, 44-45, 112, 147
Subject-object relations, 40, 58-59, 61, 84
Subsistence: see Labor, exploitation of
Supply, 100-101
Surplus value: see Labor, surplus value of

Teleology, 51, 89
Theory of knowledge: see Epistemology

Unions, 127, 144
United States, 9, 11
Unpredictable: see Marxism, as nondeterministic
Utilitarianism, 84, 109
Utopian socialism: see Socialism, utopian

Value: 65-66, 98, 102; exchange, 65-66, 82-83,
    86n, 98-99; use, 65-66, 86n, 98
Variable capital: see Capital, variable
Vienna Circle of Logical Positivism: see Positivism
Violence, 117, 126-129, 137n, 140
Voluntarism, 15, 16, 23, 24, 40-42, 46, 48, 58, 60,
    83, 132, 138

Wage-labor: see Proletariat
Wages: see Labor, wages
Welfare state, 111
Worker: see Proletariat

About the Author

Richard P. Appelbaum, Ph.D., is a Professor of Sociology at the University of California at Santa Barbara. He received his B.A. from Columbia University and his M.P.A. from the Woodrow Wilson School of Public and International Affairs at Princeton University. After serving as a technical consultant to the National Planning Office of Peru, he returned to graduate school, receiving his Ph.D. in sociology from the University of Chicago. He is the author of *Theories of Social Change* (Rand McNally, 1970), *The Impacts of Urban Growth* (with others; Praeger, 1976), *Size, Growth, and U.S. Cities* (Praeger, 1978), *Regulation and the Santa Barbara Housing Market* (California Policy Seminar, 1986), and *Rethinking Rental Housing* (with John I. Gilderbloom; Temple University Press, 1988). He has published numerous articles and technical reports on a variety of topics related to Marxist theory, urban dynamics, and public policy. His articles have appeared in such journals as *American Sociological Review, Urban Affairs Quarterly, Journal of Applied Behavior Research, Socialist Review, The Nation, Dissent,* and *In These Times*. His work has received a Chapter Award from the American Planning Association and the Douglas McGregor Award for excellence in behavioral science research.